A Pelican Book

Pelican Geography and Environmental S
Editor: Peter Hall
Townscapes

Gerald Burke is a chartered surveyor and town
planner, and holds a Ph.D. from London University.
He served with the Eighth Army in Africa and with
the Second Army in Europe during the Second World
War and was awarded the M.C. in 1945.

He was Town Planning Surveyor to the Kenya
Government and has been in consultative practice.
From 1960 he was Head of the Town Planning
Department at the College of Estate Management of
London University, moving with the College to
Reading University in 1972. He serves on
education committees of the Royal Institution of
Chartered Surveyors and has examinerships both there
and elsewhere.

A contributor to professional journals and to *Country
Life*, he was a judge for the joint Royal Institution of
Chartered Surveyors and *The Times* Conservation
Awards in 1974. His publications include two
books on town and regional planning in the
Netherlands – *The Making of Dutch Towns* (1956)
and *Greenheart Metropolis* (1966) – and, more recently,
Towns in the Making (1971).

Townscapes

Gerald Burke

Penguin Books

Pelican Books Ltd,
Harmondsworth, Middlesex, England
Penguin Books
625 Madison Avenue, New York, New York 10022, U.S.A.
Penguin Books Australia Ltd,
Ringwood, Victoria, Australia
Penguin Books Canada Ltd,
41 Steelcase Road West, Markham, Ontario, Canada
Penguin Books (N.Z.) Ltd,
182–190 Wairau Road, Auckland 10, New Zealand

First published 1976

Made and printed in Great Britain by
Butler & Tanner Ltd, Frome and London
Set in 10 on 12 pt Monophoto Times

To Peter

Read not to contradict and confute; nor to believe and take for granted; nor to find talk and discourse; but to weigh and consider.

Contents

Acknowledgements

Acknowledgement is made to the following for permission to reproduce material in this book: the Controller of H.M. Stationery Office for extracts from Ordnance Survey maps (illustrations 8 and 11); the *Architect* for illustration 48; *Built Environment* for illustration 66.

Our thanks are also due to Leicester University Press, from whose edition of Pugin's *Contrasts* illustration 30 is reproduced.

List of illustrations

List of illustrations

Preface

To many people townscape is something that has always been there, like the fields and the trees, something that cannot be readily altered and need not be altered. But townscape is made and remade over the centuries with ever-increasing investment of resources to give more efficient shelter and space for daily activities. Making it is response to known needs. Remaking it in response to known desires for change; but change involves loss as well as gain.

Townscapes never are, and never will be, finished. Some components stay virtually complete from the day the builders left the site, because to change them would be unthinkable: what, other than maintenance, could be done to improve Venice's Piazza San Marco, Rome's Piazza di San Pietro or Bath's Royal Crescent? But other components cry out to be remade: the slums of London's East End, the back-to-backs of Leeds and Bradford, and the traffic-congested and fouled streets of many an urban central area. Between these limits of what must be preserved and what must be renewed lies a range of components whose quality and usefulness is open to question in varying degrees. Study of townscapes seeks to recognize the limits of both preservation and change in relation to those components, and to consider how and when change should take place.

Study of townscapes draws upon the skills of several disciplines. Urban geography and history, archaeology, town planning, architecture, engineering, estate management, economics and sociology are prominent among them. It has attracted attention from several of them already, but remains comparatively unexplored and offers opportunity for many more studies in depth and from specialists.

The present study attempts a visual exploration of towns rather than a specialist analysis of town planning. In examining components

Preface

of townscapes inherited from various recognized periods of development it does not aspire to be a pocket history of architecture. In noting architectural successes and failures in the environment it does not aspire to architectural solutions of the kind expertly offered by Gordon Cullen, Roy Worskett and others. It notes existing methods of control over townscapes and makes some suggestions for improvement. It assesses some economic and social advantages of conservation of townscapes by reference to examples from this country and some others. But its chief aim is to increase awareness among all who are interested in the townscapes we have, and could have, and those that town councils, and developers, or both, might offer us or force upon us.

I record sincere thanks to many people who helped in the preparation of this book: to librarians at the British Museum Map Room and the University of Reading; members of the Photographic Department, University of Reading; officers in the Planning Departments of the City of London, Greater London Council, City of Westminster, London Borough of Camden, City of Coventry and County Councils of Berkshire and Hampshire; Mr F. P. Bishop, former Town Clerk of Faversham; Ir. J. Snoey and Professor Ir. J. F. Berghoef of Middelburg, Holland; Dr Theodor Hartmann and Dr Erhard Meier of Chur, Switzerland; the Royal Swedish Embassy, London; Larimer Square Associates, Denver, Colorado; David Christy and Keith Davies for their comments on the manuscript; Jill Norman and Michael Dover of Penguin Books Ltd for piloting it to publication; and, as always, to Adriana, my wife, for good ideas and good company on many a journey and for bearing with neglect at home.

1: Components of townscapes in general

We know a good landscape when we see one. We admire Nature's mountains, downland and forest, and man's fields, hedges and villages. We resent crude intrusions: the ill-sited road, buildings alien in scale and materials, the scars of mining and quarrying, the dereliction of industry.

Most of us, living in towns, do not often see landscapes in all seasons. But we see townscapes every day. Do we know a good townscape when we see one? Do we admire the forms and scale of buildings and spaces? Do we resent the eruptions of unexpected change, the loss of familiar buildings and the gain of drab slabs, the noise, dirt and danger of traffic that drives us away from streets and lanes where once we walked in relative calm? Does the pride we have in our homes extend to our towns?

Our towns are being spoiled by town councils and by town developers in both private and public sectors. We look on helplessly because, as individuals, we do not think we can do much to prevent the process. But we can. Town councils are not our masters; and they have the power to control developers. We can use the democratic process to tell our councils what we want and do not want in our townscapes. We need to present rational arguments and seek reasonable alternatives; then we need to persist until they are realized.

The word 'townscape', a newcomer to the English language, is somewhat elusive of definition. It stands for something more than the complex of built and unbuilt spaces that compose the urban landscape, the urban environment, the *genius loci*. In any British city it may arise from a medieval or even Roman core overlaid by civic, commercial and residential buildings of assorted styles and periods.

1

Townscapes

It may include Jacobean, Tudor and even earlier structures, singly or in groups, and probably much restored; seemly Georgian and Regency public buildings and terraces of houses and shops, set in avenues or around squares; ponderous and ornate mansions for the wealthy of the nineteenth century, tight and repetitious terraces of houses and tenements for the poor, and large, ostentatious but often shabby public buildings; even larger, and no less opulent, Edwardian offices, shops and hotels; and modernistic additions of the inter-war period. Post-war central and inner areas may show office blocks of considerable bulk and height, sometimes of attractive design and finish, often graceless, and occasionally brutally ugly; terraces of efficient shops lining 'pedestrian' frontages; and voluminous swathes of bungalows and semi-detached or detached houses on the outskirts. Scattered around the central business district, usually behind main streets, are numerous small workshops and yards; larger factories and warehouses surround the central core, and further outwards lie groups of modern industrial estates.

As notable as the buildings themselves is the form in which they are set in relation to each other and to the unbuilt spaces. Townscapes of ancient origin generally show an informal, irregular disposition of buildings along streets and passages and around spaces of non-geometric shape, whilst dispositions since the late seventeenth century are more formal and geometric in pattern.

Townscape can present a variety of scenes and settings – elegant, crude, distinctive, monotonous, friendly, forbidding, garish, bleak. To the man-in-the-street it is the familiar background to everyday life that may stir a vague or even pronounced like or dislike. To an observer interested in architecture and town layout it becomes more meaningful and expressive. It seldom fails to evoke some measure of response, however inarticulate or subconscious. Most British towns bear the imprint of long and mature existence. They have developed a character, an individuality, a heart. It could seldom be said of a British townscape, as Gertrude Stein observed of the endless repetitive sprawl of Oakland, California, 'when I got there, there was no there there'.

To be more than just an exercise in observation, study of townscapes must extend not only to those fashioned by our predecessors and those being made by ourselves, but to those which could be made if urban communities wanted them made. It should attempt assessments of which buildings and ground-layout forms must be conserved, which ought to be replaced, and the possible forms that replacement might take. To be effective it should also attempt costings of what must be invested or forgone in the process. Study of townscapes deserves especially urgent attention at the present time, when so much redevelopment is taking place, when significant features of the urban heritage are being replaced with scarcely any warning by the unsympathetic and the commonplace, and when such great opportunities occur for renewing and improving the visual urban environment.

Townscapes are difficult to analyse or classify; their quality is not readily measurable in any terms; what is good or bad is very much a matter of opinion. Some townscapes gained merit because they were composed by competent architects or builders, set out over fairly extensive areas, protected by restrictive covenants as to use and decorative repair, and given imaginative estate management. Such was the case with much of the speculative development carried out by Georgian and Regency landowners and investors for an affluent

1. Canterbury: war-damaged area rebuilt with flimsy-looking structures of indifferent quality, opening up a formerly narrow street and making a draughty foreground for the cathedral.

middle-class market, and equally so with New Town building by post-war Development Corporations. Most townscapes, however, took shape gradually from decisions made by individuals or authorities to develop or redevelop single sites or small groups of sites; and whilst in medieval or Georgian times piecemeal activity of this kind often achieved visually pleasing results, it has often failed to do so since then. What modern development seems to lack most is a sense of respect for the existing urban environment and for the feelings of the people whose home it is. Change has taken place at startling speed. A familiar building or a sizeable part of a street or market place can suddenly be flattened and replaced by structures quite alien to the traditions of the town [1].* Many such changes are made not because they are necessary, but because they are profitable. And what is profitable, so it seems in these days, must be right.

A town is the visible expression of the collective activities and attainments of its inhabitants. As the furniture and furnishings of family homes give an insight into various individual levels of wealth or poverty, of good taste or lack of taste, of pride of possession or indifference, so the design and disposition and juxtaposition of buildings and spaces in a town reveal collective characteristics and qualities. But whereas homes tend to reflect the standard of living enjoyed by individuals at the present time, augmented in varying measure by inherited possessions, the town as a whole reflects the activities and building achievements not only of its present inhabitants but also of their predecessors, sometimes of many generations.

In varying degrees, townscapes are also a reflection of the many interacting influences that brought about the location and aided the growth of urban settlement. Geography, topography, climate and economic *raison d'être* were original dominating influences. Also significant were the quality and quantity of building materials obtainable in the locality; the skills in design and building craftsmanship available at particular times; and those peculiar accidents or actions in history whereby some towns gained status as seats of government, seats of learning, sees of bishops or places of pilgrimage, or were chosen instead of others, apparently for no compelling technical reason, as centres for industry, manufacture or commerce.

* Figures in square brackets refer throughout to the numbered illustrations.

Components of townscapes in general

The influence of geography, especially in regard to ranges, valleys, rivers, harbours and fertility of soil, on the location of urban settlement needs no emphasis here, except to note the decisive influence of navigable rivers and overland routes on the development of towns.[1] Riverside towns tended to grow in lines parallel to the main stream, with factories and warehouses along the banks and commerce and the market place on higher ground behind, preferably near a road bridge: witness Kampen, the handsome Dutch port on the Ijssel river, or Bewdley, small, compact and centred on the riverside and roadbridge. River-trade routes linked by canals during the second half of the eighteenth century gave rise to canal-side architecture, warehouses especially, showing the combination of grace and utility that was so characteristic of the period; and at least one town, Stourport, owes its existence to and derives its graceful form from a canal.

The system of Roman highways in this country, and of minor roads feeding into them, linked the earliest settlements and created many more. The Ordnance Survey Map of Roman Britain shows that town locations were seldom far from highways and often astride them. Towns of Roman or medieval origin located at a cross-roads, a bridge, a ford, alongside a river or at a confluence of streams tended to develop common structural forms which produced townscapes of structural similarity but of varying appearance, dependent upon the locality in which they were situated. Later forms of transport, notably the railway, brought significant structural changes, *inter alia* by orienting the central business district of a town towards the main-line station or stations; and the subsequent decline of rail in favour of road transport was often reflected in reorientation towards the medieval market place and high street.

The most pronounced expression of town pattern, town shape and townscape arises from topography. The flat site tended to encourage the setting out of orderly building sites of rectangular shape, served by roads on a grid pattern and readily divisible into house-plots or shop-plots of standard sizes. This was normal practice for towns that had to be built in a hurry, as by a conqueror or colonial power wishing to defend and exploit newly annexed territory: standardized plot sizes were administratively convenient for fixing rents and taxes. By contrast, the hilly site of asymmetrical shape was unsuitable for

Townscapes

a formal layout pattern but encouraged an 'adaptive' form of layout, whereby the largest available flat sites were reserved for the most imposing public buildings, leaving smaller buildable areas for less significant components such as houses, shops and workshops. In ancient Athens, the classic example of adaptation of buildings to irregular topography, pride of place was accorded to the Acropolis, with the Parthenon and other temples crowning the dominating plateau; tiered seats for theatres were hewn out of the hillside beneath; the *agora* occupied gently sloping ground with surrounding building-groups linked by broad flights of steps; temples and official buildings took other prominent sites; and houses, workshops and other humbler structures stood in clusters in between.

The imposition of formal, rectangular patterns on flattish or evenly sloping sites tended to produce uniform and rather dull townscapes. This is true of nineteenth-century industrial towns, of formal Renaissance towns, of medieval 'planted' towns ('bastides') and of the many planned 'colonial' settlements developed during the long march of Roman empire-building and the much earlier Macedonian and Hellenistic expansionist periods. 'Adaptive' growth, by contrast, produced townscapes of informality and variety.[2]

Closely allied to land form, as a factor in the moulding of towns and townscapes, is climate. Although seldom misunderstood or neglected by ancient or medieval town-builders, climatic factors were often underrated or ignored by their successors, and particularly so during the present 'enlightened' century. The most pleasantly habitable urban environments usually proved to be those designed and built to suit prevailing climatic conditions. For town-building in hot and dry conditions, the ancients learned that main streets set out in the direction of the prevailing wind enabled stagnant warm air to be drawn out from narrow streets and lanes, and that water in 'tanks', or shallow open pipes or streams alongside streets, could help to humidify a dry atmosphere. Streets seldom followed straight alignments for long distances lest high winds should raise the dust excessively. Houses for such climates were oriented so as not to face the fierce western sun: their rooms, with small openings to minimize glare, gave on to an inner courtyard to maximize shade as well as privacy. The arrangement of larger houses around two courtyards

6

2. Harlow: Bishopsfield/Charters Cross: unconventional layout (1961) of L-shaped patio houses in double rows on either side of footways; flats and maisonettes around hill-top podium, garages below; density approximately 90 habitable rooms per net acre.

afforded morning shade to one and evening shade to the other. Layouts such as these, which were adopted for Mohenjo-daro and other major cities of the Indus Valley civilization of 3250 BC, are still common in modern India and other countries with similar climates. The resulting townscape or 'streetscape' was somewhat unfriendly and secretive, presenting only a door and possibly a small, high window to the street elevation. Such streetscapes are still typical of many Eastern towns (for example the Casbah in Algiers or the narrow streets of Zanzibar) and they have counterparts in modern versions of 'patio' housing, as, for example, in Harlow New Town [2].

Mild and sunny climates encourage community life in the open air. Greek and Roman citizens spent much of their day in the *agora, forum, palaestra* and baths. Medieval man in Mediterranean lands used the tree-lined town square and sheltered market places as his places of business and trade, and the town fountains or wells provided his sources of news and gossip as well as his daily water-supply. Open squares and tree-lined avenues served also as places for business and social exchange in Renaissance times.

Towns in cold and wet climates arose on sites protected from prevailing winds, avoiding north-facing slopes to make the most of orientation. Their buildings huddled close; tall structures observing irregular building lines and overhanging narrow streets and paths, as at York's Shambles or Canterbury's Mercery Lane, broke the force of gusty winds and gave some shelter from rain and snow. Hearth and home were the refuge for cold days; the townsman in temperate or cold climates looked inwards to his family rather than outwards towards the community: not for him the lively outdoor existence, with social activity continuing far into the night, that was, and still is, typical of warm and sunny climes.

Climate loomed less large as a factor in town development as

3. *Chipping Campden: curved High Street flanked by limestone buildings of seventeenth and eighteenth centuries; market hall, 1627. Note scrappy repairs to footpath at left.*

Components of townscapes in general

engineers gained increasing technical competence and confidence in
countering the forces of nature. Layout of buildings and streets came
to be decided more in terms of economy in services – water reticulation, drainage, sewerage, gas and electricity – and of achieving the
maximum density of accommodation than of securing the ideal
orientation for maximum sunlight or protection from the prevailing
wind. Gas and electricity for heating and lighting could compensate
in some measure for exposed siting or poor orientation. But disregard
of climatic conditions usually meant decrease of habitability.

In recent years when urban development or redevelopment took
place very quickly, on a large scale, at a high density, and using
untried building materials and technology, neglect of micro-climate
produced some unexpected results. Developments comprising tall
blocks interspersed with terraces of two to four storeys gave rise to
unforeseen and greatly intensified gusts when the wind blew from a

*4. Warwick: Mill Street: timber houses (c. 1600) which survived the great fire of
1694; the three-gabled house in the centre is nineteenth-century.*

Tow*scapes

particular direction. In consequence, fountains that were intended to
bring cool buoyancy to the scene could suddenly soak unsuspecting
passers-by; pedestrian precincts that were intended to offer a pleasant,
traffic-free, open-air environment tempting shoppers to linger and
gossip could suddenly be assailed by a near-tornado, buffeting all
within range and sending paper, cartons and skirts awhirl. Several
such precincts, among them the Merrion Centre at Leeds, had to be
roofed over in order to continue in use.

Townscapes were, and often still are, an outgrowth or result of a
country's geological structure. The rich variety of building materials
yielded by Britain's well-defined geological regions established typical
forms for building and typical colours and textures in various parts
of the landscape.[3] Some towns and, more so, villages still proclaim
from the house-tops their deep-rootedness in the locality. No visual
harmony can quite equal that deriving from buildings in a landscape
constructed from the materials of which that landscape is composed.

Cotswold towns [3] and villages, among many others in the limestone and clay belt, assert the prevalence of oolitic limestone. The
Peak District displays local gritstone not only in nearly every building but in nearly every garden wall, gate-post, stile and field boundary.
Tough granite defies the severity of winter in Scotland and Wales and
the gales in Devon and Cornwall. Cumberland's identity is in plastered
stone and thatched roofs. Dispersed parts of the clay belt produced
bricks of a variety of colours and textures. Chalklands accounted for
flints, sometimes used with brick or stone quoins, and for a range of
materials, including white plaster, to infill timber-framed construc-
tions [4]. The Weald and Greensand belt is characterized by timber-
framed structures with brick nogging or hung tiles or weather-
boarding. North Norfolk could be recognized for its knapped flint,
as could southern East Anglia for its elaborate pargetting. Building
craftsmen created equally localized characteristics in the many ways
in which they combined or used materials – chequerboard flintwork,
alternate bands of brick and flint, patterned slate and shingle roofs
and walls – as well as in details of design for porches, doorcases,
fanlights, pediments, bargeboards and a host of other features.

These and other strongly accentuated regional and local building
traditions became blurred, and in some cases virtually vanished, when

10

5. *Egham: Royal Holloway College (1879–87), an ebullient Victorian complex modelled on a sixteenth-century French Renaissance château.*

canals and, later, railways facilitated the transport of mass-produced bricks, slates, tiles and other components to all parts of the country in response to heavy demand for cheap housing from a rapidly increasing population. W. G. Hoskins describes this process, first quoting from a book on Middlesex.

'From 1850 onwards' – with the triumph of the railways – 'every kind of material was poured on to the unprotesting soil: harsh red bricks, sometimes glazed; in the north, yellow-green brick from the Three Counties, near Hitchin; slates, pantiles, green tiles; stucco, artificial stone and concrete.'[4] What happened in Middlesex eventually happened all over England, and as Midland bricks and Welsh slates – and later more unspeakable materials like asbestos and corrugated iron – flooded into every corner of provincial England, the ancient local materials that fitted their own regions so well, for they came out of their very soil, disappeared one by one. In Oxfordshire the Stonesfield slate-pits and mines shut down one by one during the second half of the nineteenth century; in Leicestershire the Swithland slate-quarries, which had been worked since Henry III's time, shut down altogether in 1887; and so it was in nearly every county in England. All regional styles and all local materials were exterminated except where the well-to-do could afford to build deliberately in the old manner, with the aid of an architect. What had been the living style of a whole region, modified to suit all classes of people, became a piece of pleasant antiquarianism for a rich man.[5]

Hoskins's reference to 'extermination' of local styles is fortunately something of an overstatement. Despite the unabated changes wrought over the past two centuries by industrialization and rapid increase of population, much of this pre-1750 regional and local accentuation survives as a recognizable element of today's townscapes. Much survives, too, of building materials beloved of the Victorians: cast and wrought iron and glass that enclosed with astonishing skill the vast loftiness of main railway stations, exhibition halls and conservatories; stucco, terra-cotta and glazed tile surfaces, and stained glass in windows and door-panels, and a superabundance of ornamentation applied to their buildings great and small [5].

Twentieth-century townscapes are expressed in no very strong or positive styles, but in a variety of forms that varies with the sizes and uses of the buildings in question. Suburban housing areas occasionally show some recognition of local materials and building traditions, but in town centres new buildings constructed of reinforced concrete or steel frames and clothed with prefabricated units or claddings usually outstrip their neighbours in size to make profitable use of the sites. Modern central areas sometimes gain new and imaginative additions, but too often the structures are unscholarly, repetitious, utilitarian units – Betjeman's 'rent-collecting slabs' – that seem to owe more to the creativity of an accountant than an architect. Raw concrete surfaces, shiny and highly coloured plastic panels and prodigal areas of glass framed in chromium or aluminium, are the predominant accents of twentieth-century townscapes [6], whilst traditional materials are often used in untraditional ways and out of sympathy with particular locations.

In addition to physical factors so far considered, townscapes also derive in part from a complex succession of events in history that helped to influence the lives of townspeople, their faith in the supernatural, their means of making a living and sharing it with less fortunate brethren, their artistic aspirations, architectural skills and constructional achievements. Fortuitous events or political decisions

6. London: South Bank slabs, with St Paul's Cathedral at extreme left.

in history may still be reflected in some of the outward signs that contribute to the 'character' or 'individuality' which every town acquires for itself over the years.

Such events could cause a city such as Canterbury to become a place of pilgrimage, or a city like Winchester to gain status as the Norman capital of the Kingdom and to lose it to London some centuries later. It could cause some towns, rather than others apparently equally suitable, to become bishoprics and thence grow to importance as centres for secular regional government, or some towns to be founded as offshoots of monasteries and to develop either because of monastic influence (Abingdon, Evesham) or in spite of it (Coventry, Reading). Some ancient university towns remained comparatively unscathed by the growth of industry or commerce in the vicinity (St Andrews, Durham); others retained venerable and mature townscapes at the centre but took on unexpectedly modern ones on the outskirts (Oxford, Cambridge). Some towns that were successful as medieval market centres were all but swamped visually by the nineteenth-century surge of industrial and commercial expansion (Birmingham, Manchester, Leeds, Sheffield); others that failed to be chosen as industrial centres or main railway junctions succeeded at least in retaining much of their pre-nineteenth-century urban character (Stamford, Nantwich). There are towns that gained wealth from the woollen industry in medieval times and lost it after the eighteenth century, retaining a wealth of historic townscape (Bradford-on-Avon); others in the same industry gained even greater wealth in the nineteenth century but lost on quality of townscape (Bradford, Yorks.). Among towns that performed essentially the same function, some show similarities in appearance (Eastbourne, Worthing), others differ markedly (Brighton, Blackpool).

These and other similarities and differences arising from individual decisions, royal patronage, town councillors' ambitions or industrialists' whims highlight the intricacies in attempting to find rational explanations for forms of townscape. More subtle contrasts arise when it is appreciated that townscape regarded merely as a physical composition is as inanimate as a theatre stage without the players. It is the people going about their daily affairs who bring life to the urban backcloth; the people as well as the buildings reflect urban character; the people as well as the buildings emphasize the contrasts between Winchester and Wigan, Salisbury and Salford, St Albans and St Helens. Buildings and people combine in presenting scenes: vivacity, as at a seaside resort in high season and full sunshine, or the same on a wet afternoon in winter; contrasting age-groups in and out of term in a university city or a 'school town' – Oxford, Cambridge, Eton, Marlborough; sedateness in a cathedral city; austere solidity in a large industrial town; the cosmopolitan look of King's Road, Chelsea; the comparative social uniformity in a New Town shopping centre. These are, of course, superficial and generalized observations, but none the less valid in essence.

Nor are townscapes immutable. Although the main framework of roads, footpaths and alleyways and the boundaries of building plots may well endure for centuries with no pronounced alteration, the buildings and spaces may quite frequently be replaced, renewed or adapted to meet new demands or realize new potential in land values. Changes of a temporary nature are also created by advertisements on hoardings, billboards, shop fascias and windows, and in multi-coloured neon strips or bulbs. The people bring changes too: new fashions and colours in clothes and accessories and carrier-bags continually bring colour and movement to what might otherwise be a drab urban scene.

Left till last in this preliminary consideration of factors that influence townscapes are the two that pose the greatest menace to traditional forms: the rapid increase in population experienced by many cities and towns since about 1830; and the phenomenal and continuing rise in the number of motor vehicles using urban roads, especially since the 1950s.

Growth of urban population, which nineteenth-century industrial and commercial enterprise made possible and twentieth-century developments sustained and increased, led to a corresponding increase in demand for floor-space for industries, offices, shops and homes. This in turn raised demand for redevelopment of existing sites and development of new ones at higher densities, and for more land for development for all urban purposes. In central business districts, old buildings on key sites that did not represent economic use of site value were demolished and replaced with buildings of much greater capacity. Densities of development in such districts increased greatly; tower blocks and slabs of offices and new parades of shops shot up in likely and unlikely places, bringing startling changes to skyline and street elevations. Residential areas spread further outwards: high-density flats and maisonettes punctuated the periphery, and large and small estates of houses covered huge areas of land in outer districts. The speed of development over the past quarter of a century has been so swift as to bring bewildering, even alarming, changes to the familiar built environment, and no small resentment towards those people who benefit from them from those who do not.

The motor vehicle brought equally startling changes.[6] The townsman on foot needs compact grouping of buildings and reasonably narrow and safe streets and footways to enable him to move easily and conveniently around and across any locality, for example a central business district. The townsman on wheels requires wide, straight, unobstructed streets for rapid and direct journeys, convenient accessibility to buildings for loading and unloading of goods,

7. Los Angeles: Hollywood freeway and Civic Centre. Some two thirds of the land area is devoted to the motor vehicle, at rest or in motion.

and adequate parking space as close as possible to his destinations. Pedestrian townsman and propelled townsman are in a state of continual conflict which even frequent interchange of roles does not resolve.

Traditional towns built for man on his feet, and modified for man on horseback or in a horse-drawn carriage, observed appropriate relationships between height and bulk of buildings, width of streets and footways and dimensions of squares and other public places. Such relationships produced townscapes with a sense of continuity and enclosure sympathetic to the pedestrian. Towns designed on the basis of maximum convenience for man on wheels inevitably observe an entirely different set of relationships, with broad belts of carriageway sweeping across, over or under the urban area for the vehicle in motion, and huge parking areas for the vehicle at rest [7]. It is impossible to find the additional urban space required for these purposes if existing towns and cities are to retain anything like their traditional form. To give high priority of access to the motor vehicle, most traditional towns would have to be virtually taken apart and rebuilt over a far more extensive area.

These varied facets of townscape need further exploration in later chapters; but even a superficial examination leads to the conclusion that inherited townscapes are at serious risk at the present time. Modifications and additions to the existing fabric very often introduce features that are unfamiliar, unworthy both of our urban tradition and of our creative abilities and technical skills. The future form of townscapes is still apparently being left largely to chance. Despite the efforts of those who attempt to control development it is frequently in the hands of developers with little concern for townscape and no stake in the towns, other than the profit to be gained from rapid redevelopment of selected sites.

It is obviously necessary to see the subject in perspective. Urban development and redevelopment cannot be viewed solely as an exercise in aesthetics. Only in rare instances can townscape be equated with fine art. Only rarely can buildings be treated as masterpieces. Towns are made to be used and lived in; buildings are made to serve the particular purposes for which they were designed. A town originally built for horse-drawn transport is unlikely to be suitable for the motor vehicle. A building designed for clerks with quill pens may not be readily adaptable for use by workers with typewriters or computers. Towns and buildings must respond to compelling changes in modes of living, working, travelling and recreation; but such changes do not necessarily have to be met by wholesale destruction of inherited urban assets and replacement with entirely new forms. Gradual change is possible; and an understanding of how to introduce urban change sensitively lies at the heart of any sound policy relating to townscape.

2 : Medieval and Renaissance components

There is something very enduring about a town layout, whether it be one that took shape from a preconceived plan largely implemented within a decade or so, or one that grew spontaneously from a small nucleus in response to varying demands for accommodation over the centuries. Setting out boundaries for house plots, laying foundations for buildings, and constructing roads, footpaths and water supply, drainage and sewerage systems, even to very simple engineering standards, established patterns that persisted sometimes over many centuries. Replacements for buildings that collapsed, or perished in fires, or gave place for redevelopment, nearly always arose on the same plot and on the same foundations as their predecessors. Although from time to time streets were widened and their building lines adjusted, they nearly always kept much the same alignments. Market squares and other open 'places'* which acted as settings for churches, guildhalls or other prominent buildings altered comparatively little over the centuries, although their areas were often reduced by encroachment of buildings in permanent materials replacing temporary market stalls. The central areas of many towns in Britain and Europe arise from a virtually unaltered medieval pattern of streets and house-and-garden plots.

It is surprising how closely ancient cities that were more or less continuously inhabited throughout the centuries still adhere to their pre-medieval layout patterns. For example the nucleus of Turin (and

*In town-planning jargon the word 'place' is taken to correspond with the French *place*, German *platz*, Italian *piazza* etc., i.e. 'an open space in city or town usually surrounded by buildings'. The English word 'square' is nearest in meaning though a 'place' is not necessarily four-sided or right-angled.

to a lesser extent those of Chester or Colchester) still echoes the formal lines of a classical Roman colonial town; Paris still shows the *grande croisée* of Roman roads across the Seine and Île de la Cité; London's City, still defined by its Roman wall, is disposed around an essentially medieval pattern of streets, alleyways and courtyards; and even monstrous modern Manhattan has scarcely departed from the ground-plan devised for it in 1811.

Although, however, the layout forms of ancient cities and towns may have remained substantially unaltered, the same cannot be said of the building masses and elevations that later arose from them. Urban communities continually change their built environment by modifying or replacing parts of the existing fabric, or extending it, often on a large scale, over previously undeveloped or under-developed sites. In medieval times the built environment underwent sudden and violent changes caused by fires, which could devastate large areas and necessitate rebuilding at frequent intervals. Towards the end of the seventeenth and throughout the eighteenth and early nineteenth centuries, urban environments were enlarged by extensive and profitable projects of town houses in a variety of sizes and prices, promoted by landowners and speculators to satisfy an apparently inexhaustible demand from an affluent middle class. In the heyday of nineteenth-century industrial Britain, commercial and industrial development was concerned to accommodate new techniques in mass-production of goods, bulk storage of materials and merchandise, and maintenance of detailed records and filing systems. These called for purpose-built factories, warehouses, exchanges, exhibition halls and the like. Mass housing for the rapidly increasing population of workers was also needed as close as possible to factories, mills and 'works', and at minimum cost in land, building materials and services.

The process of industrialization and the rapid spread of buildings for all purposes transformed many an urban topography by destroying trees, hedges and other vegetation, flattening hills and filling hollows, raising embankments and slashing cuttings, and canalizing or culverting rivers and streams. New methods of transport brought especially drastic changes. The railway transformed much of the urban environment with lines, stations, goods yards, marshalling yards, tunnels, viaducts, bridges, engine-sheds, and so on. Continued industrialization and expansion during the twentieth century with even newer forms of transport brought equally far-reaching economic, social and visual changes. The internal combustion engine accounted for highways, motorways, flyovers, underpasses and parking lots. Increased population and wealth brought buildings of massive scale – office-blocks, hospitals, hotels, schools, blocks of flats and the like – displacing small buildings on small plots. So townscapes are continually evolving; those that remain comparatively unaltered are usually in places that make little economic advance in the modern world.

The many long-established towns of a long-inhabited land like Britain are thus a complex of layout forms and building styles of many ages. Each age has swept away much of its predecessors' work; but each age has also allowed ancient features to survive. Some endure because of their intrinsic beauty; others because of their historic association with great events or great people; others again because of the sheer effort entailed in pulling them down (a Roman amphitheatre, or medieval castle, or town gate). Some survive only partially in the original condition as, for example, former Georgian houses along a high street with shop extensions built on their former front gardens, or with ground-floor windows and doorcases replaced by plate-glass and internal walls removed to give modern display-space. But most survived because their design, accommodation and construction are still of sufficiently high quality to permit of useful service today.

Essential aims in studies of townscape should therefore be to recognize and evaluate the quality, individually and collectively, of buildings from the past, to assess their architectural merit and their setting and to find appropriate uses for them. It is also necessary to discover what communities of this age want for their urban environment and the price they are prepared to pay, in effort and money, towards maintaining and improving it.

Most modern British townscapes can claim few direct links with a past much more than ten centuries old. Compared with such towns as Orange, Nîmes, Arles and Trier, where superb theatres, amphitheatres, temples and town gates give a memorable continuity with a classical Roman past, the British classical heritage is meagre indeed. Rare fragments such as the denuded theatre at Verulamium, the stunted amphitheatre at Dorchester, the walls and gates at York, Canterbury and Chester (overlaid by medieval masonry and over-generously restored by nineteenth-century enthusiasts) and traces of pavements, floors, baths and hypocausts in scattered localities, are of little significance in townscapes. In indirect links, however, our urban environments are enriched by buildings with forms and details derived from the classical past, whether by applied decoration directly copied from original creations or from various Renaissance versions of original designs. Doric, Ionic, Tuscan and Corinthian motifs, and the essential features of a Roman temple such as the famous survivor at Nîmes, appear time and again in diverse forms and sizes in public buildings of all kinds – town halls, churches, museums, concert halls and art galleries – as well as in palaces and stately homes.

The earliest components of our townscapes which do have direct links with the past usually belong to the long medieval period, which started with the Normans and faded into the emerging classicism of the Renaissance towards the end of the reign of Elizabeth Tudor. Medieval townscapes arose from two distinct forms of settlement. The 'planned' or 'planted' form[1] was built virtually as a single undertaking over a period of five to ten years, in accordance with a plan prepared for the particular site. The 'adaptive' or 'organic' form[2] grew gradually over the centuries, at times rapidly but usually slowly, as the demand for accommodation dictated.

'Planned' towns had been introduced on a small scale by the Normans, but many came into being in the great wave of new-town foundation, sweeping over Europe during the twelfth and thirteenth centuries, that left hundreds of settlements in its wake. The need to protect and exploit newly annexed territories led kings and con-querors to grant land to nobles, as landlords, for the foundation of new towns and villages. The landlord commissioned a contractor to prepare a site-layout plan, set out the wall and/or moat defences, streets, lanes and building plots, and also to find tenants to build and occupy houses, and farm or otherwise work the surrounding land. Tenants gained security of occupation in return for covenants to erect a building of approved type within a stipulated period, commonly two years, and to pay an annual duty. The landlord retained control over the uses to which plots could be put, the buildings to be erected and the plot coverage. The normal requirement was that the building should extend over the whole street frontage, sharing party walls with neighbours, but ample garden space remained at the rear. The landlord also reserved sites for the church, market place and various community buildings.

Most of these new-town foundations (called variously *newton, novus burgus, nova villa, villeneuve, neustadt, nieuwstad*, etc., but known in town-planning jargon as 'bastides') were set out on a rectangular grid pattern with main streets about 25 feet wide and minor roads 16 feet, giving frontage to building plots, and 8-foot lanes at the rear. The street grid defined building blocks capable of subdivision into about a dozen building plots typically 24 by 72 feet. Two building blocks or *chequers* near the centre of the grid were normally reserved for church and market-place respectively.

The church, town hall and possibly some guildhalls and leading citizens' houses were built in permanent materials, sometimes brought at considerable cost from distant quarries, by skilled building tradesmen. The ordinary citizens' houses were built with materials locally available, mostly timber for framing, plaster for infilling and thatch for roofing, though later brick, stone and tiles came into use. Methods of construction were sufficiently straightforward for families and neighbours to build for themselves with the minimum of skilled assistance. Townscapes developing from such settlements were seldom artistically remarkable; yet they showed a sense of order and seemed at one with the landscape, being formed largely of the same materials.

Bastides built by kings, such as Louis IX's Aigues Mortes on the Mediterranean coast or Edward I's Winchelsea on the Sussex coast, were usually fortified at great cost with brick or stone walls, gates and watch-towers; others founded by nobles with smaller resources might have little more than earth banks and ditches for protection. Characteristic of numerous Welsh bastides, in particular those built at the order of Edward I, was the modest little settlement nestling at the foot of a massive castle. Caernarvon, Beaumaris and Conway

[8] are three examples in which the castle still dominates a grid of narrow streets lined with buildings of small scale, closely packed within high walls punctuated by watch-towers. Only one British bastide grew great: Edward's port of Hull is now swamped by prosperous development. Most of the others are small towns; Winchelsea is hardly more than a village and still has many undeveloped chequers; and many foundations in Wales have disappeared without trace and are known only from written records.

The 'adaptive' or 'organic' form was typical for medieval towns: the bastide was the exception. The adaptive town kept pace with the needs of its community, expanding with increase of numbers and prosperity, marking time or declining with other economic or political changes. Its shape and arrangement of buildings, streets and

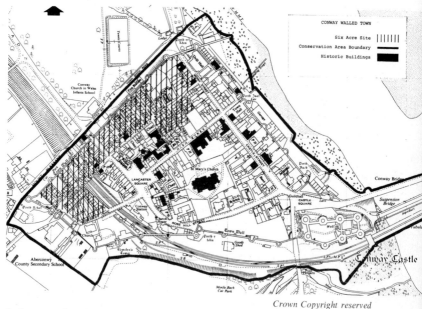

Crown Copyright reserved

8. *Conway: plan of 'bastide'. Distance between Upper and Lower Gates 1,000 feet. High Street 25–28 feet wide, plot frontages on average 15–25 feet and depths about 90 feet. Cottages on hatched area (6 acres) are to be rehabilitated for use by holidaymakers.*

23

alleyways reflected the character of the site, whether hillside, river-side, seaside, roadside, ford or crossroads. The shape of house plots was less regular than in bastides. They resembled the cultivated strips in the fields beyond: long and narrow, with frontages some-times barely 10 feet wide and depths of 100 feet and more [9]. In some cases, on sloping sites especially, urban strips were not recti-linear but had curved sides. These narrow plot frontages had their influence in giving a vertical accent to buildings and townscapes generally, as will be seen later.

The medieval urban communities of landowners, merchant- and craft-guildsmen, labourers and peasants attached little importance to planning the future development of their towns; urban popula-tions increased only slowly over the years and town councils saw no need to provide for significant expansion. They were content to find space within the walls for additional houses, workshops, storehouses, guildhalls, roads, harbours, bridges or other develop-

9. *Northampton: narrow frontages (second from left scarcely 12 feet wide) along west flank of market place, giving vertical accent to the buildings; see also 11.*

10. York: Stonegate: at left Mulberry Hall dated 1434, jettied, oriel windows on upper floors; at right typical eighteenth-century shop and house with pedimented middle window.

25

ment as and when needed. If pressures on available land within the walls became too great, 'suburban' growth took place outside or, if the situation required it, the town limits were extended and new walls built.

Houses, workshops, barns and other buildings varied in size and type of accommodation but shared a 'family likeness' and stood together as good neighbours because they were all constructed in the way most suited to local building materials. Thus some medieval townscapes would comprise mostly half-timbered structures with overhanging storeys necessarily supported on jettied beams [10], whilst others in brick or stone would normally show flatter and more regular elevations. Roofs of thatch, slate or tile were pitched to suit the climate of the region: steep for northern countries to allow easier run-off for rain or snow, flatter for sunnier, warmer regions. Roof-lines in Scandinavian and Mediterranean countries emphasize this difference.

In contrast to the orderly, rectangular bastide, whose straight streets of buildings could be taken in at a single glance, the characteristic 'adaptive' medieval town showed little evidence of any but short-term planning. Seen on a town map, the arrangement of streets, alleyways, house plots, buildings and spaces appears illogical and inexplicable, with streets meandering in confusing courses, changing frequently in direction and width and sometimes coming to dead ends. The building blocks bounded by such streets and alleys were often much larger than those of a bastide, so that the interior of a block could accommodate occasional small terraces of houses facing on to long, narrow alleyways or set around quiet, planted courtyards. The market place and other principal built-up 'squares' were usually of irregular shape, as also were the numerous small 'places' that occurred here and there as if by chance at a junction of streets or footways, or a set-back of buildings along a street.

The apparently haphazard pattern is only meaningful when it is appreciated that the medieval town grew very slowly, and its inhabitants were not a homogeneous mass but a series of families and small groups, each making its distinct contribution to the life of the town. Families and groups with common interests tended to congregate in the same districts, and to arrange their environments to accord with their own particular activities. Thus builders of houses, workshops and storehouses would set aside spaces for local communal purposes – small 'places' for the fountain, or local market, or other meeting place. Identity of economic activity was the principal *raison d'être* for these local communities within the urban community as a whole. The fact that similar crafts and trades tended to congregate in the same quarters or streets is shown by place-names still surviving in many towns, large and small. The heart of London still has its Bread Street, Friday Street, Paternoster Row (for makers of rosaries), Leather Lane, Ironmonger Lane, and many others.

Of special significance in the medieval townscape was the arrangement of buildings in and around public 'places' or squares. At the heart of most towns the 'market square' [11], to which many routes led, served not only for trade but also as the setting for plays, processions, proclamations and public gatherings of all kinds. All but the smallest towns had at least two, sometimes more, such open places, some of which gave stature to important buildings such as the town hall or guildhalls, while others might accommodate additional market places for commodities in which the town specialized, such as cattle, fish, cheese, wool, flax or linen. These spaces could be formed by setting buildings back on one or both sides of a main street, or by setting aside a wide space for the purpose.

As with the Greek *agora*, and especially the Roman *forum*, medieval 'places' were systematically enclosed by buildings. The built frontages, occupied in the principal town 'square' by the town hall, guildhalls and important shops and offices, or in smaller 'places' by specialist shops, market buildings, houses or workshops, showed a pronounced sense of continuity and enclosure. Although several streets and passages gave access to the square from all sides, their entry upon the square was contrived to cause minimum interruption to the continuity of building frontages [11]. The sense of visual enclosure thus achieved was welcome in a place which played so important a part in community activities and which, in some respects, was a substitute for the classical *odeon*, the theatre or amphitheatre. The enclosure was also physically

Townscapes

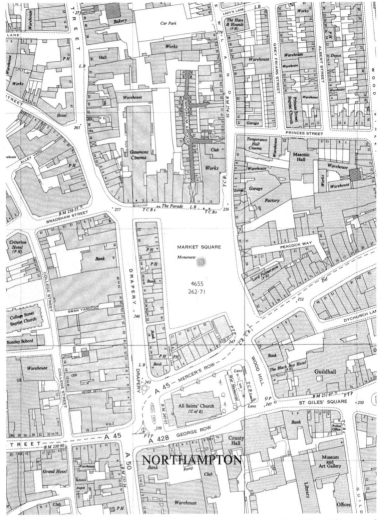

11. *Northampton: OS map of market square. Note dimensions (nearly 200 feet deep and 20–25 feet wide) of building plots on western side of Drapery; note also the continuity of building frontages around the Square, interrupted only by three streets and four narrow passageways.*

welcome, since it excluded cold winds, or at any rate broke their force.

A notable feature of the medieval town square was that its centre was almost invariably kept open and unobstructed by fixtures such as market crosses, fountains, statuary and other adornments. Adornments there were: but seldom so placed as to clash with everyday activities. In praising and advocating such an arrangement, Camillo Sitte[3] noted the analogy of children choosing places to make their snowmen:

> These snowmen stand in the same spots where … monuments or fountains might be expected to be located. How did this placement come about? Very simply. Imagine the open square of a small market town in the country, covered with deep snow and criss-crossed by several roads and paths that, shaped by the traffic, form the natural lines of communication. Between them are left irregularly distributed patches untouched by traffic; on these stand our snowmen, because the necessary clean snow was to be found only there.
>
> On exactly such spots, undisturbed by the flow of vehicles, rose the fountains and monuments of old communities.

The medieval 'adaptive' townscape showed continual variety and contrast. There were contrasts of scale, as with small houses nestling at the foot of a cathedral [12] or tall church, or as between the imposing town hall, guildhalls and leading citizens' houses around the chief squares or along wide streets, and smaller houses and shops along narrow streets or alleys leading off the square or High Street. There were contrasts of decorative quality, as between the materials and craftsmanship lavished on a splendid Gothic cathedral which took centuries to complete, or on a church, guildhall or wealthy citizen's house, and the primitive standard of most burgesses' homes. In the environment the animation and noise in public places and thoroughfares contrasted with the sequestered calm of a cathedral cloister, university quadrangle [13], or courtyard of almshouses.

The medieval urban environment and townscape, an informal association of individual buildings compactly grouped to form enclosed spaces, arose from a developing fabric ideally suited to a

12. *York: Stonegate: timber-framed, jettied and rendered fifteenth-century houses at left; elegant late-eighteenth-century shop-front with statue of Minerva on the cornice; also glimpse of Minster.*

13. *Cambridge: Corpus Christi quadrangle, late fourteenth century.*

community which moved around mainly on foot. The harmonious relationship of man with his environment stemmed not only from a compactness that gave ready accessibility from all parts of the town to the centre, but also from the visual satisfaction that enclosed spaces could offer. Moving along a meandering street, flanked by buildings which adhered to no regular building line but formed sometimes convex, sometimes concave and sometimes straight frontages, a pedestrian would encounter a continually changing succession of visually enclosed spaces, each differing from the others. As one building façade passed out of view, so another would quickly appear. Here, a minor road flowing into the street [14] would disclose a vista in some depth; there, a small 'place' at the side of the street might unfold another view in breadth. Every few paces would bring a slight change, or possibly a sudden revelation of an imposing structure such as the cathedral, church or town hall. The urban scene, if not always endowed with architecture of distinction, was almost always distinguished by visual variety and sometimes by picturesqueness of a high order.

The Renaissance in town planning,[4] which had its roots in fifteenth-century Italy, introduced entirely new forms of townscape, all of which differed from characteristic medieval forms in at least

31

14. Zurich: typical medieval street, lined with buildings of modern date; 'footscape' poorly maintained.

two notable respects. First, the medieval townscape was a compound of individual units that could normally be seen a few at a time and close at hand; the Renaissance townscape was typically a series of compositions of buildings and related spaces, each comprising individual units that had been standardized and integrated into a single *tableau* or a disciplined succession of related *tableaux*. Second, the medieval townscape showed a series of flat elevations which changed in appearance in slow or rapid succession as the observer moved along a street or across a built-up space; its Renaissance counterpart was a composition in depth, such as a long straight avenue or a forecourt to a cathedral or palace, not unlike a stage set enclosed on three sides [15], and capable of being observed and comprehended at a single glance.

The Renaissance approach to urban design was a methodical, even mathematical, development of the newly discovered classical formality of ancient Greece and Rome. The revived orders of archi-

15. Greenwich: Wren's hospital buildings (1696–1750) symmetrically arranged about the central axis of Inigo Jones's Queen's House (1618–35).

33

tecture, Doric, Ionic, Corinthian, Tuscan and Composite, appeared in designs for large public buildings and palaces. The remains of temples, theatres and other classical creations, meticulously measured and analysed, inspired new architectural forms and new groupings of buildings. New interpretations of architectural proportion and scale, and of the use of space about buildings, emerged in many a treatise,[5] on many a drawing board, and on many a newly developed site in city and town. The device of perspective, derived from contemporary paintings, was enthusiastically adopted for displaying buildings and associated features to greatest effect.

In contrast to the irregular and piecemeal development of a typical medieval 'place', Renaissance *piazze* were of regular, geometric outline, mostly rectangular, though sometimes with opposite sides diverging to heighten the effect of perspective. Later versions in Italy incorporated semi-circular, oval or other formal shapes, e.g. Piazza di San Pietro, Rome. Designers strove to secure sympathetic relationships between the length and breadth of the *piazza* and the heights of buildings surrounding it. While no set rules were prescribed, it was often the case that the height of the tallest buildings would define the minimum length of the longer side; thus a *piazza* dominated by, say, a tall church would be made at least as long, or possibly up to twice as long, as the height of the church itself, while the length of the shorter side would bear a similar relationship with the heights of buildings on the longer sides.

Fountains came to be regarded as decorative rather than utilitarian features and, together with statues, obelisks, columns, arches and other sculptural and architectural adornments, were treated collectively as components in a total composition instead of as individual features of utility, beauty, or both, in their own right. Statues, in particular, lost much of their individual meaning: their placing was such as to gain artistic effect for the whole conception, to mark the geometric centre of a space [16], to delineate a major or minor geometric axis, and to act as visual magnets in drawing attention to particular vistas. Thus they stood in draughty isolation, divorced from the buildings or settings with which their subjects would have been associated. Churches lost still more of their meaning and status. Some designers treated them with arrogance as mere architectural elements

Medieval and Renaissance components

16. *Brussels: Place Royale: late-eighteenth-century formality. St Jacques Church (1776–85) is the central feature of one flank; the statue of a Crusader hero marks the geometric centre of the square.*

in an impressive *tableau*, instead of with reverence as sacred elements in a secular setting.

This preoccupation with architectural effect rather than function is well emphasized in the splendid Piazza del Popolo, Rome, designed to give a noble entrance to the Renaissance city. A new city gate, Porta del Popolo, was erected in 1561, and an extensive slum clearance to the south enabled the straightening of two avenues and the creation of a third to afford improved lines of travel from the gate to the inner city. An Egyptian obelisk was re-erected in 1589 to mark the precise intersection of the prolonged axes of these three avenues; to mark their actual point of arrival on the south side of the *piazza*, two symmetrical architectural features were added (1662–7) on either side of the middle avenue. These features were churches of identical design and detail whose individual function as places of worship was subordinated to their artistic function as components of architectural adornment and balance. Grand designs of this order were made for a

35

distant future. It took several decades to implement plans for the Piazza del Popolo, while its present form, with elegant curved boundaries to east and west, was conceived and implemented by Guiseppe Valadier as late as 1816–20.

As the new order of design progressed, its main tenets took clear form. Streets were to be straight, and visually terminated at each end and at intersections of important routes by specially designed architectural or sculptural features placed precisely on the centre-lines to 'frame the vista'. Streets leading into a *piazza* or forecourt would follow alignments that had been precisely determined in relation to dominant buildings or monuments. Building-façades in streets or *piazze* would be continuous and, as far as possible, of uniform height. Building lines would be strictly adhered to in insuring orderly development along streets. *Piazze* would retain geometric shape, and building-façades surrounding them would conform to prescribed lines in respect of fenestration, doorcases, string courses, cornices, copings, balustrades and other features. The unit of design was the whole street or square, rather than the individual building.

Two new factors emerged towards the end of the sixteenth century to influence the shaping of Renaissance townscapes. The first, originating in Italy, spread to northern Europe during the seventeenth century and further afield thereafter. This was the fashion for creating large-scale ornamental gardens,[6] not only for relaxation and pleasure but also to afford an elegant setting for palaces and large country houses. Because so many sites in Italy tended to be steeply sloping, the terrain had to be shaped into a series of level terraced plains, linked by balustraded stairways and subdivided by a system of broad avenues and paths into inter-linked lawns and ornamental flowerbeds (parterres) of various geometric shapes. Planting of all kinds was strictly regimented: trees were drilled in open and close order, and lopped and trimmed to sculptural shapes; shrubs and flowers paraded in intricate formations. Canals, lakes and pools were defined by rigidly geometric banks, and fountains spurted symmetrical streams.

Parks and gardens of this kind, set out at much greater scale over the broad plains of France and Spain, and to slightly smaller scale in Stuart Britain, covered extensive tracts of land and created landscapes of beauty and grandeur. The greatest exponent of formal 'landscape architecture', as it came to be known, was André le Nôtre, creator of the grandest park ever made: Versailles, which was commended with unrestrained enthusiasm by J. C. Loudon:

...the grand scale and sumptuous expense of his plans surpassed anything before seen in France... His long clipped alleys, triumphal arches, richly decorated and highly wrought parterres; his fountains and cascades, with their grotesque and strange ornaments; his groves, full of architecture and gilt trellises; his profusion of statues and therms: all these wonders springing up in a desert-looking open country, dazzled and enchanted every class of observer.[7]

Each formal park or garden comprised essentially a framework and the spaces contained within it. The framework was expressed by broad, tree-lined avenues, prolonged sometimes over great distances, intersecting at *rondpoints* and terminated by architectural or sculptural features such as garden 'temples', summer-houses, arches, obelisks, columns, statuary and fountains. The spaces within the main framework were planted with a variety of trees, shrubs and flowers, adorned by sculptural and other features, and further subdivided by minor avenues and paths. Each of the spaces in the garden could be made to display individual characteristics in much the same way as a pattern of streets, paths, buildings, spaces and planting could confer a particular character on various parts of a planned town. A close relationship gradually developed between garden planning and town planning: the framework of avenues and paths, the long vistas, the monumental terminating features, *rondpoints* and parterres were echoed in the long, straight streets intersecting at roundabouts; the spaces corresponded to *piazze* and residential and other areas in planned or 'improved' cities and towns. The resemblances which plans of Versailles, Hampton Court, Badminton and many other formal gardens bear to the plans of Washington DC, New Delhi and Canberra are unmistakable.

The other factor that brought change to Renaissance townscapes was the increase in urban traffic, first horsemen and then horse-drawn carriages. Travel over greater distances and at higher speeds required streets with straight alignments, more gradual curves, easier gradients, wide carriageways to speed the movement of non-pedestrian traffic, and separate footways for the safety of pedestrians.

Greater speed, and the increased height from which buildings could be viewed from a carriage, also called for new forms of building along avenues. Hence there developed the so-called 'architecture of the carriageway', typified by uniform, flat, parapeted façades, punctuated rhythmically by rows of windows and doors, and visually enclosed by decorative, and at times monumental, buildings or sculptural features at street intersections and terminations (e.g. Pulteney Street, Bath). In course of time the façade assumed such importance in the composition of a street or 'place' as to be designed, and even built, first, the accommodation being tacked on to the back as required. Hardouin-Mansart adopted this procedure for building the elegant Place Vendôme (1699) in Paris; and John Wood used it for Queen's Square (1730) and for the Circus (c. 1755, implemented by his son) in Bath.

Some Renaissance towns and townscapes were designed in plan and elevation as complete entities and built within a comparatively short span of years. This was true of 'ideal cities' designed by architects, artists, philosophers and military engineers from the mid sixteenth century onwards in Italy, France, Holland and elsewhere on the European mainland.[8] The artistic inventiveness and versatility of the age produced a lively range of geometric patterns, from the radial-concentric style as at Mariembourg (1550) and Philippeville (1555) in the Namur province of modern Belgium, at Palmanova (1593) in Italy and Coevorden (1597) in Holland, to a succession of variations on the rectangular theme as at Sabbioneta (c. 1570) and Leghorn (c. 1575) in Italy, Willemstad and Klundert (1583) in Holland, Charleville and Henrichemont (1608) in France and Freudenstadt (1599) in Germany. All were developed with buildings mostly of modest scale but having orderly, rhythmic façades such as those that still enclose the market place at Charleville or line the 'miniature Champs Elysées' at Willemstad.[9] Britain has no 'new towns' of sixteenth-century date. Whitehaven (started 1660) and Stourport (1795) are among the very few new foundations of pre-nineteenth-century date.

The Renaissance 'new town', like the medieval bastide, was an exceptional rather than normal form of urban development. Although architects and their patrons knew well how to build new towns in ideal conditions, existing towns were usually well located in relation to trade routes, and also represented considerable capital investment that could not be lightly dispensed with. The most successful achievements in early Renaissance townscape were the large-scale improvements made to well-established cities, notably those that were seats of royal or aristocratic government.

Improvement did not necessarily require the razing of large areas of medieval development and the imposition of an entirely new ground plan. It entailed a measure of demolition to remove congestion, to allow freer circulation of traffic, and to clear warrens of slums that might harbour threats to peaceful government, followed by replacement with individual buildings and groups in the new classical styles. Local rulers sought to create scenes of beauty, even of grandeur, that would impress not only their subjects but also influential visitors from other cities or countries seeking to establish or extend trading relationships. Owners of urban estates saw good prospects for investment of capital in building houses, workshops and warehouses, and they undertook such development whenever it seemed profitable to do so. Although not averse to clearing away existing buildings – and their inhabitants – if it could be done without undue difficulty, they usually found it quicker and less troublesome to build on open land, such as the gardens of a large house, or fields formerly used for grazing cattle within the town walls.

Improvement schemes in Italian cities of the fifteenth and sixteenth centuries sprouted and blossomed to produce townscapes of ordered formality. At first the building forms echoed the symmetry and flat façades of classical Greece and Rome, but later in the sixteenth century the flowing curves of façades and the sweep of balustraded stairways showed the dynamism and splendour of Baroque ideas. Florence set the pattern with Brunelleschi's Foundling Hospital (1419) in the Piazza Annunziata, and followed with other classical, symmetrical forms for churches, palaces and public buildings, arising mostly from a virtually unaltered medieval ground plan.

In Venice, the magnificent Piazza San Marco began to take shape from 1480 onwards with the building of the three-storey palace along the north flank. In Mantua, various localities were graced with buildings designed by the great Leon Battista Alberti; in Ferrara a new quarter to the north, laid out in rectilinear style (c. 1495), included four elegant palaces at the intersection of the two main streets; the splendid palace at Urbino also appeared about this time. In Genoa (c. 1550) came the archetypal Renaissance avenue, the Via Nuova (later Via Garibaldi), lined with palaces and houses for the nobility and designed as an architectural unit with strict observance of a standard top cornice-height of about seventy feet. But excelling all in monumental grace were the improvements and extensions in the 'Rome of the Popes' wrought by Michelangelo, Bramante, the Fontanas, Bernini and other masters of architecture and sculpture. The *piazze* del Campidoglio, del Popolo and di San Pietro are eloquent of this style of townscape.

17. Paris: Place des Vosges (1607–12), classic enclosed residential square; closed corners, streets entering through archways to avoid interruption of façade. Area of enclosed space nearly 6 acres.

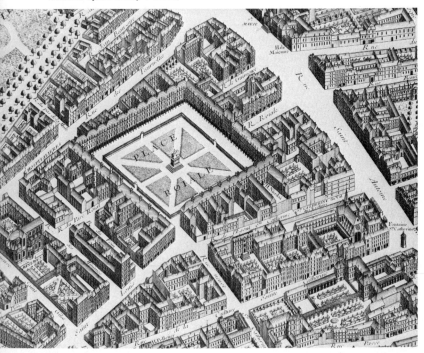

These brilliant expositions of monumental urban design, which drew visitors from many countries – not least the English noblemen and country gentry on the 'Grand Tour' – inspired similar developments in the rest of Europe and, later, in the New World. In the Paris of that astute royal developer Henri IV came admirable prototypes of residential squares – Place des Vosges (originally Place Royale, 1607–12) [17] and Place Dauphine. The Place des Vosges was set out on the site of a large house and garden as a spacious quadrangle flanked by uniform three-storey terraces of elegant façade with continuous arcades at ground level giving a pronounced sense of enclosure; the only two streets entering the square did so through the arcades, thus causing no visual interruption in the façade. At the mid-points of the north and south sides the elevations were slightly heightened to mark the axes and avoid monotony. The central space was planted as a formal garden for the benefit of residents, whose houses had no private garden-space but only small backyards. An equestrian statue of Louis XIII, erected towards the end of the seventeenth century, took typically Renaissance pride of place at the geometric centre of the square. This still admirable investment set a precedent in speculative town-housing development for the wealthy; its counterparts are to be seen in many European cities, and not least in British developments of the late seventeenth, eighteenth and early nineteenth centuries.

Henri IV's widow and the Regent of France, Marie de Médicis, inspired the city's first tree-lined avenue, the stately Cours-la-Reine, extending for a mile alongside the Seine's north bank and leading into the Place de la Concorde. This broad, densely planted, well shaded feature soon found favour as a meeting place for fashionable society, on horseback or in carriages, and also set a pattern for similar projects elsewhere. The additions made to the Paris townscape by Henri's grandson, Louis XIV, were a byword in monumental splendour including as they did much of the Louvre, the Hôtel des Invalides, the Tuileries gardens, the Place Vendôme, the Place des Victoires, the Grands Boulevards and, above all, the superb Avenue des Champs Elysées.

Monumental urban design was also much in evidence in Renaissance Spain. Madrid's Plaza Mayor (completed 1619), an enclosed colonnaded square resembling Paris's Place des Vosges, provided not only 136 houses with balconies for witnessing bullfights and other spectacles, but also accommodation for the town bakery, butchers' shops and guilds of clothiers, silk merchants and other traders. It was thus a popular meeting place for the community. In common with France and Italy, however, most of the best of Spain's secular Renaissance townscape was created for the benefit of monarchs and aristocrats rather than for the ordinary citizen.

Although Sir John Summerson has detected signs of the Italian Renaissance in the detailing of certain English buildings dating from as early as 1528,[10] its earliest expression in terms of British townscape is owed to our first classical architect, Inigo Jones (1573–1652).[11] Early in the seventeenth century Jones had accompanied his patron the Earl of Arundel on a tour of Italy which included visits to Florence, Rome, Naples and Genoa. Taking for his 'guide-book' a copy of Palladio's *Quattro libri dell' architettura*, he was able not only to study Palladio's ideas and designs (themselves derived from Alberti and thence back to Vitruvius) but to examine in detail the Master's original drawings for palaces, churches, villas and other commissions, to see the completed buildings in Venice, Vicenza, Udine and elsewhere, and to discuss them with one of the Master's famous pupils, Scamozzi. He also measured the dimensions and studied the proportions and details of many remains of buildings of Roman antiquity. Thus steeped in the new classicism and imbued with enthusiasm to practise it, he returned home in 1615 to the appointment of Surveyor of the King's Works.

In this influential capacity he lost no time in introducing the Renaissance into British townscapes. It was a slow process. His first new buildings, the Banqueting House in Whitehall (1619–22) [18] and the Queen's House at Greenwich (1619–25) [15], were of a style so utterly different from prevailing Jacobean, Elizabethan and Tudor styles as to provoke dislike and mistrust. Gradually, however, his architectural innovations – unity and symmetry, large regularly spaced sash windows, porticoes, pediments, columns, pilasters, balustrades and the rest – impressed the King and interested potential developers.

From one speculative developer (the Earl of Bedford), with per-

18. London: Banqueting House (1619–22) by Inigo Jones. Rigidly symmetrical, three centre bays accentuated by columns (Ionic at first floor and Corinthian above) and side bays by flat pilasters; first-floor windows with alternate segmental and triangular pediments, garlanded frieze above second-floor window; roof concealed by balustrades.

mission from the King and skilled design from Jones, there came London's first formal Renaissance square. Covent Garden 'piazza', built 1631–5, comprised a rectangle some 450 feet by 300 feet with the long side oriented approximately north-east. The plan in Colen Campbell's *Vitruvius Britannicus* shows continuous arcades with no buildings behind on three sides and St Paul's Church, flanked by two linked houses, on the fourth, western, side. Houses were later built behind the arcaded façades on the north and east sides but not on the south, which was bounded only by a wall because the Earl would not sacrifice the garden of his house which adjoined the square. St Paul's Church was in the tradition of a plain and powerful Tuscan temple, seeming to preside over the square as a classical temple might have dominated a typical Roman forum. The inner rectangle of the Piazza, surrounded by low posts, was adorned by a small obelisk at the precise centre. Although the houses ('fitt for habitacions of Gentlemen and men of ability') attracted some wealthy tenants, as did the Place des Vosges in Paris some twenty years previously, its prosperity as a residential square was short-lived. By 1670 part of the central space was in use as a market, and gradually the whole area was taken over as London's whole-sale fruit and vegetable market. Little remains of the original houses; but the decision taken in 1968, and implemented in 1974, to remove the market may yet give that part of London a proud architectural asset.

Covent Garden Square was the precursor of several estate development schemes which gave London a succession of elegant and profitable squares of town houses, many of which survive in their original form, though not always as residences. Lincoln's Inn Fields, developed after Jones's death in accordance with a ground plan he prepared, has a pair of houses (nos. 59 and 60), probably of his design, which served as a model for town housing in many hundreds of streets and squares of the eighteenth century and after. Other seventeenth-century squares include Leicester (1635), Bloomsbury (1665), Soho (1681), Red Lion and St James's (1684) and Grosvenor (1695).

Successful estate development of houses and associated buildings in the new classical style was by no means confined to London. The whole country had been enjoying increasing prosperity under the Tudors and early Stuarts and, as wealth accumulated, especially in the ports and well-placed market towns, a surge of building and rebuilding brought new elements to the urban scene. Town houses, shops and warehouses commissioned by merchants, and churches, town halls, market halls, corn exchanges, schools, almshouses and other buildings of classical form, set in surroundings of predominantly timber-framed construction, brought sharp contrasts of townscape. The surge abated during the Civil War, but gained new and greater impetus after the Restoration.

Landowners and speculative builders found another outlet for their energies in a new form of urban enterprise that emerged early

19. *Tunbridge Wells: The Pantiles, seventeenth-century shopping group which allows no frontage access to wheeled traffic; street lighting from lamps attached to buildings; well-maintained 'floorscape'.*

in the seventeenth century. London was considered no place for the monarch and fashionable society to remain in all the year round, particularly during the summer, and medicinal springs were proving useful in relieving the diseases of the rich; thus the inland health resort came into its own. To relieve an exclusive clientèle of visual and social boredom it was necessary to provide not only elegant and comfortable residences, but also shops, hotels, eating-houses, assembly rooms, gambling-houses and other meeting places of high quality. That Tunbridge Wells [19] and Epsom were among the first to gain popularity early in the seventeenth century is still attested by surviving individual buildings and urbane groups. Bath and Buxton were prominent, and grew apace, during the eighteenth century, while Cheltenham, Leamington, Harrogate and Scarborough flourished in the Regency period. The health 'spa', together with the seaside resort that succeeded it in the late eighteenth and early nineteenth centuries, made a notable contribution to the legacy of the best in British townscapes.

Christopher Wren, Jones's great successor, had no direct experience of the developing Renaissance townscapes of Italy. His only visit abroad was to France, although he probably learned much about Italian cities from meetings with Bernini in Paris. His designs for large public buildings seem to show greater affinity with French than with Italian versions of the architectural Renaissance; his designs for houses clearly reflect a liking for the elegant, unpretentious Dutch houses of the seventeenth century; but his own inventive mind and outstanding abilities in artistic and structural design evolved a characteristically English Renaissance architectural style.

This is not the place to consider his masterpieces, including London's St Paul's Cathedral and fifty-two City churches, or to speculate upon how London's townscape might have appeared had his brilliant plan for rebuilding after the Great Fire of 1666 been implemented. Suffice it to say that his inspiration, and that of his pupils, associates and successors, Hugh May, Nicholas Hawksmoor, James Gibbs, John Vanbrugh, William Kent and others, brought new elegance and delight to cities, towns, villages and countryside. Wren's own 'fusion of classic grace with vernacular energy', added

to Jones's Palladianism, brought a fine progression of public buildings such as town halls, university colleges, schools, hospitals, almshouses, market halls, customs houses and churches.

Although none of the several plans for redevelopment of the City
after the Fire proved acceptable to the King or the Council, the
disaster had one important outcome for townscapes. The Act for
the Rebuilding of the City of London, 1667, introduced comprehensive building regulations that put an end to the casual practice of
medieval and Tudor times. It standardized development by requir-
ing the use of brick or stone walling and tiled roofs, and specified
the number of storeys to be built in streets of differing widths and
importance. Implementation of this Act resulted in a controlled
urban form with regular frontages, building height related to street
widths, uniformly spaced windows and related string courses and
cornices. In John Summerson's words:

> Never before had such sweeping control of building activity been
> entered on the Statute-book. The whole of the houses to be built in the
> new City were divided into four classes, 'for better regulation, uniformity
> and gracefulness'. In the 'high and principal streets' (six only were classified
> as such) houses were to be neither more nor less than four storeys in
> height; in the 'streets and lanes of note', three storeys was the rule; while
> in 'by-lanes' two storeys were prescribed. A fourth class was reserved for
> 'houses of the greatest bigness', which did not front the street but which
> lay behind, with their courtyards and gardens. In practice, a good deal of
> freedom was exercised in the distribution of the various types, since it was
> obviously impossible to classify London's streets and lanes in a hard and
> fast manner. But that the result was satisfactory is proved by every illustra-
> tion of the City streets, which shows that they achieved a reasonable
> orderliness without monotony.[12]

The Act helped to reinforce the high standards already in use by
speculative builders at the time, who were active in the West End
of London. Their clients were mostly middle-class merchant
families; the poorer class was concentrated in less expensive dwellings to the north, and especially to the east, of the City boundary.

The small 'Queen Anne' house which proved so appropriate in
town, village or countryside, soon became a familiar feature of
townscape and landscape [20]. It was built to a simple rectangular

20. *London: Nos. 11 and 12 Kensington Square, c. 1685. Typical small semi-detached houses, 'Queen Anne' (more accurately 'Wren') style; basement for kitchen and servants, ground floor for dining and other reception rooms, first floor for salon and principal bedrooms, second floor for bedrooms, attic for servants; good brickwork, tiled roof, stuccoed string courses; door hood on corbels, sash windows on bracketed sills; moulded dentils, pedimented dormers.*

Medieval and Renaissance components

plan and symmetrical façade, in two or three storeys with attic accommodation for servants. Local materials – brick or stone and tiles – were invariably used, and the elements seldom varied: tiled roof concealed by parapet, small dormers, evenly spaced sash windows and attractive doorcase headed by a canopy with straight or curved pediment, or deep, rounded hood often of shell pattern. The interior had well-shaped rooms, often panelled, with decorated plaster ceilings, and classical motifs in chimney-pieces and architraves. Few houses of the time, whether for rich or poor, were without individual or shared garden-space at the rear. Such buildings, in terraces, in semi-detached pairs or detached, arranged loosely around a village green or compactly along a town street or around a square, greatly enhanced the quality and value of the built environment, and set a pattern for the great Georgian and Regency periods over the succeeding century and a half.

The Renaissance in British town planning was seldom expressed in terms of building new towns on sites previously undeveloped, or of massive extensions to existing towns; rather it involved gradual and orderly additions on fields or gardens, or in replacement of medieval slum districts. The extent and character of such additions or redevelopments were closely geared to prevailing demand and the availability of development finance. At times they were quite considerable and rapidly executed, especially if resulting from widespread fires; at other times they amounted to hardly more than a couple of streets or squares, completion of which might be delayed for many years if demand contracted or development resources dried up. Most residential development was financed by speculators on land leased from a private landlord or city council for a long term, usually ninety-nine years. The fortunes made by the notorious Nicholas Barbon [21] in three post-Fire decades of speculative building spurred others to similar enterprise.

Georgian taste in architecture, publicized by such works as Colen Campbell's *Vitruvius Britannicus* (1717–25), Leoni's edition of Palladio's *Quattro Libri* (1715–16), James Gibbs's *Rules for Drawing the Several Parts of Architecture* (1732) and various copy-books for builders, soon made its impact all over the country.

To draw an analogy between Georgian townscape and a well-

21. *London: Buckingham Street: No. 17, at right, by Barbon (1675), doorcase typically eighteenth century; No. 18 has Corinthian pilasters and a straight hood on covered brackets, and elegant ironwork.*

managed stage performance, individual decorative public buildings took honoured places as principals, but the success of the show as a whole stemmed from the powerful backing of an elegant and competent chorus and orchestra of well-planned speculative housing. And corresponding to the unseen crowd of stage-hands and administrative staff were the mews dwellings for ostlers, coachmen and others, as well as long terraces of small houses for the 'working classes'.

Insistence on the use of permanent building materials for reconstruction in London after the Fire had stimulated the production of bricks in great quantities and at sufficiently reasonable cost to enable their standard use for new work in many districts. Brick, which had proved so suitable for building in the Queen Anne style, was no less so for succeeding Georgian versions. Subtle variations in the properties of local clays, together with differing skills among brickmakers, produced a rich assortment of colours and textures – 'as many different varieties of brick in England as home-made loaves' – although red was the predominant colour in southern and Midland counties. Limestones, sandstones, granite and other materials continued in use in districts where they were readily available. The two greatest single achievements of comprehensive development in eighteenth-century Britain – Bath[13] and New Edinburgh[14] – were constructed mainly in limestone and granite respectively. Nevertheless, building in brick predominated throughout the Georgian era; and nowhere more comprehensively than in the splendid streets and squares of Dublin [22].

The typical Georgian town house was a standardized product made from standardized mass-produced windows, doors and other components. Accommodation on each of (usually) three main floors comprised four rooms, two at the front and two at the back, arranged on either side of a central staircase, with a small room or closet sometimes included in a projection at the back. For terraced housing, entrance hall and staircase were often placed at the side. Servants' quarters were tucked away in mansard attics screened by parapet walls, or in basements poorly lit and ventilated by narrow windows just above ground or, later, giving on to narrow yards fronted by railings. Externally, the standardized plan was echoed in standard-

22. Dublin: Merrion Square, late eighteenth century. Comparative uniformity of building façades saved from monotony by a variety of doorcases and ironwork at first-floor level. Elegant lamp standards of nineteenth century.

ized elevations which nevertheless allowed for a measure of variety in the detail of the various components. Twelve-pane sash windows with delicate glazing bars were tall and slightly narrow, spaced at rhythmic intervals, slightly recessed, and headed by 'flat arches'. Doorways, with fanlights sometimes of exquisite patterns, were surmounted by curved or flat projecting hoods carried on carved consoles or, later, by pediments or friezes supported on pillars or pilasters. Projecting cornices rested on modillions. Roofs were partially concealed behind parapets or balustrades. Wrought-iron gates, railings and balcony balustrades [22] drew the houses into a closer unity and heightened the sense of rhythm. Town houses were almost invariably constructed in long terraces flanking straight streets, squares and, later, 'crescents' and 'circuses'. The Georgian façade became so highly regarded as a status symbol that it was often grafted on to robust medieval, Tudor or Jacobean town houses [23]: many a fine classical front to be seen today all but conceals a main structure of considerably greater age.

23. Faversham: No. 5 Abbey Street has a three-storey eighteenth-century façade with parapet roof planted on to a sixteenth-century structure; first and second floors converted as one large room; handsome doorcase with Doric columns and pediment.

Equally efficient and well-mannered were Georgian shop premises, whether developed in complete streets, like Milsom Street, Bath, or in smaller but related groups in small towns, especially those reconstructed 'all-of-a-piece' after widespread fires – Woburn [24], Blandford, New Alresford and Wareham are examples. The shopfront was as pleasing as the houses it served. Spacious display-windows, sometimes large and flat, sometimes small and sharply bowed, larger and more gently bowed [25], or with a flowing serpentine curve, were set out on either side of an elegant doorway, with the door glazed to match the windows. Above the doorway or windows a fascia bore, in delicate lettering, the proprietor's name and business; occasionally a fixed or hanging sign gave a sample of the standard of workmanship that could be expected in goods sold or services rendered. Towards the end of the eighteenth century shop-fronts had become a popular subject for copy-book designs: I. and J. Taylor's *Designs for Shop Fronts*, London, 1792, included elegant examples.

Georgian and Regency architects could also respond more than

24. Woburn: market place, rebuilt after a fire in 1728; shop-fronts of late eighteenth century.

adequately to demands for industrial buildings. Their breweries, factories, warehouses, canal-side architecture and river- and sea-docks (for example London's impressive St Katharine Docks or the mill at Bromley-by-Bow [57]) were, in general, structures which met operational requirements without pretence or conceal-ment of purpose.

This large-scale, well-controlled town growth continued through-out the period of the Regency until the third decade of the nine-teenth century. It is not possible here to pursue its various phases and characteristics, from the neo-classical revival, expressed with re-strained elegance by the brothers Adam [26] or in more ebullient form by Sir William Chambers, to the picturesque 'Gothick' style inspired by James Wyatt. But one contemporary creator of noble townscape should not go unnoticed. The work of John Nash, em-bracing both the neo-classical and the picturesque, is memorable, possibly more for its quantity than for its intrinsic quality. With sup-

25. York: No. 37 Stonegate. Elegant eighteenth-century bow shop-front, richly carved console brackets supporting carved fascia; fluted Corinthian columns at side entrance, all painted black to set off the silver and jewellery on display.

port from the Prince Regent, who put at his disposal extensive areas of Crown land, and from Parliament, which facilitated the acquisition of other land needed for implementation of his plans, Nash was able to do in some measure for London what the Woods had achieved for Bath, and Craig, Reid and Sibbald had achieved for Edinburgh.

This was more than estate development: it was town planning and town development which included not only residences for a well-to-do middle class and housing for artisans and workmen, but also accommodation for commercial, entertainment, cultural and other purposes. The Marylebone Park Estate project produced a wide swathe of noble townscape extending eastwards and northwards from Westminster via splendid shopping streets to some delightful suburban villa development in what later became Regent's Park. While building was in full swing at the northern end, starting

26. *London: No. 7 Adam Street, c. 1775; elegant doorcase, giant pilasters with honeysuckle decoration, plain pediment and elegant wrought-iron balconies.*

in 1812 with the stately curves of Park Crescent, linking to James Adam's imposing Portland Place and thence fanning northwards to Park Square and the grand terraces around the Park, Nash was quietly acquiring in small parcels the additional land required for the 'New' (now Regent) Street which was so vital to provide for shopping and through traffic. A shrewdly selected location for this fine thoroughfare, along the western edge of semi-slum property in the Soho district, achieved the dual benefit of comparatively low acquisition costs and ready access westwards to fashionable estates which had been developed during the previous century.

Nash did not succeed in securing firm architectural control over the scheme as a whole because he could not command sufficient capital to finance the development of such an extensive area. Instead he was obliged to make blocks of land available to investors for development, and later to piece the frontages together, as best he could. He did gain uniformity in one respect by using, and encouraging others to use, white stucco as a rendering [27]; he was also personally responsible for many of the plans and elevations and supervised others. The key feature, which he reserved for his own creation and financed from his own resources, was the magnificent Regent Street Quadrant, completed by 1823. However, it lost its famous colonnades in 1848 and was extensively remodelled in Edwardian times. The whole grand enterprise, embracing Waterloo Place, part of Piccadilly Circus, Suffolk Street, Carlton House Terrace, Buckingham Palace and the ground plan for Trafalgar Square, was virtually complete by the time of Nash's death in 1835.

The activities of this adroit and successful architect and estate developer were not confined to London. He designed country houses, picturesque villas and cottages, prisons for Welsh towns, and elegant terraces, crescents and squares, notably in Brighton and Hove. Possibly his best-known work outside the capital city, Brighton's fantastic Royal Pavilion, enabled his royal master to imagine himself in the role of eastern potentate extraordinary.

Early Renaissance townscapes, as already noted, reflected the symmetrical forms of layout used for parks and gardens; a similar relationship appeared when new ideas for garden design came into fashion at the beginning of the eighteenth century. The formal garden was at its most extravagant under the Stuarts and at its most artificial under William and Mary. Tyrannically geometrical layout, meticulously detailed planting, crippling maintenance costs, and 'much neatness without the least Nature', brought the inevitable reaction. The new movement in landscape design, seeking to 'copy Nature unadorned', to eschew straight lines, geometric patterns and flat planes, succeeded in creating informal scenes and 'prospects to excite not only the eye but the imagination'. The development of these ideas in the individual interpretations of the early masters Charles Bridgman and William Kent, the enormously popular 'Capability' Brown, devotees of the Picturesque such as Richard Payne Knight and Uvedale Price, and the versatile Humphrey Repton, need no further description here. What is of interest is the effect of this 'landscape school' on townscapes.

The effect was twofold. First, it brought informal, 'natural'

27. *London: Strand: 'pepper-pot' towers at either end of the West Strand Improvements planned by Nash and built 1830–32. Only the original façades now remain: the interior has been gutted for redevelopment* (1975).

arrangements of trees, shrubs, flowers and lawns into the urban environment. The gracious Georgian squares, conceived originally as terraces around a paved central space, gained greater grace as oases of green amid built-up areas. On the larger scale, towns gained the great benefit of parks, developed from royal property, from common land, or from the former gardens of large houses. William Kent's first brilliant essay in informal garden planning, at Chiswick House, London (c. 1740), was not opened to the public until quite recent times, but his replanned Hyde Park has been a joyous feature of townscape for several centuries. So, too, has St James's Park, originally set out by Inigo Jones and replanned a century and a half later as part of John Nash's 'Royal Mile' development by his then partner Humphrey Repton.

Secondly, the principles of design of a 'landscape school' garden had their influence, if somewhat less obviously, on the actual layout of urban roads and spaces. The meandering footpaths and the elements of 'surprise, variety and concealment' in the placing of sculptural and other features in such a garden had been in evidence centuries earlier in the picturesque, informal dispositions of streets and buildings in 'adaptive' medieval towns; but these characteristics were not consciously applied to modern towns until the late nineteenth and early twentieth centuries, when Camillo Sitte demonstrated their delight and relevance.[15] Raymond Unwin, writing in 1909,[16] noted how the typical form of a landscape garden was echoed in the structure of residential extensions at Bournemouth, Eastbourne and Buxton, where roads followed contours and gave access to house sites affording maximum advantage of orientation and view.

In these and other instances, the rigid rectangular grid of streets, beloved of public health engineers as ideal for reticulation of water supply, sewerage and other piped services, gave place to a less formal arrangement. Streets curved with the contours and met each other at 'T' junctions instead of at direct crossings, and building lines allowed for the occasional set-back of houses to give small open spaces for trees, lawns and other planting. Houses served by such roads could be so sited as to give a lively, changing street scene, instead of long uniform terraces and corridor streets rigidly ruled by building lines.

Townscapes

Unwin himself applied such devices in layout plans for Hampstead Garden Suburb and Letchworth Garden City, which still offer much inspiration and many a lesson for makers of modern residential townscape.

3: Victorian and Edwardian Components

The controlled townscape that characterized the long Georgian era was the product of happy combinations of circumstances. New development was often comprehensive, covering extensive areas of land in single ownership and conforming to an estate master-plan. Although developers may have envisaged it as 'full of gentry of distinction, their houses proportioned to their station', they did not aim their investment solely at the middle-class market. Dwellings were included for servants, artisans and workmen, and accommodation was provided for horses and carriages. (And what a boon that accommodation would have been in meeting garaging and parking needs today – had not much of it been later converted to mews flats and bijou *pieds-à-terre*!) Development made use of local building materials, which expressed an individual sense of 'place', and of standardized windows, fanlights, doorcases and other components, which expressed a universal sense of 'period'. It represented what architects like to call a vernacular architectural language: a style ordained by a few arbiters of elegance and followed without question by builders and occupiers, even to the acceptance of specified colours for external walls and openings. It made an admirable environment for people who, for the most part, journeyed neither far nor often from their town, and who were not yet exposed to an industrial economy that demanded urban sites for large factories and mills. It grew steadily, hastening slowly, to accommodate a steadily increasing population.

Townscapes of the nineteenth century were formed in less propitious circumstances. The power to build was gradually passing from the *ancien riche* to the *nouveau riche* – from owners of large landed estates, accustomed to planning and building on a large scale for a distant future, to owners of much smaller parcels, who were motivated more by short-term needs. Development during the first half of the century nevertheless continued to be on quite a large scale. In cities and towns that bore the immediate brunt of the Industrial Revolution, especially those mining coal and iron, or manufacturing metal, pottery, woollen, cotton or other mass-produced goods, or serving as markets, entrepôts and ports, new development was rapid and extensive, but not coordinated by town planning control.

As more factories and mills took up central urban locations, bringing, mostly by immigration, a sudden increase in working population, so batches of high-density working-class dwellings were run up as close as possible to them. As the urban environment grew more noisy, polluted and congested, driving middle-class families out to suburban districts, so batches of low-density villas spread over green fields. The vacated middle-class town houses, sometimes in good Georgian terraces and squares, deteriorated in multi-occupation by poorer families. Thus began the sharpening of segregation between employer and employee and the erosion of a sense of community in towns. A contemporary observer of Manchester noted:

> The separation between the different classes, and the consequent ignorance of each other's habits and condition, are far more complete in this place than in any country of the older nations of Europe, or the agricultural parts of our own kingdom. There is far less *personal* communication between the master cotton spinner and his workmen, between the calico printer and his blue-handed boys, between the master tailor and his apprentices, than there is between the Duke of Wellington and the humblest labourer on his estate, or than there was between good old George the Third and the meanest errand-boy about his palace.[1]

New mass-produced dwellings for workers tended to present a dreary monotony of appearance that derived from non-local mass-produced brick and other building materials, now readily transportable by canal, river barge or railway truck to most parts of the country. The back-to-back slums covering vast areas of Birmingham, Manchester, Leeds, Bradford or Nottingham, into which people were packed at more than a thousand per acre, need no elaborate description here. Nor does the strait-laced uniformity of 'byelaw' housing emanating from the Public Health Act of 1875.

Implementation of this epoch-making Act had an immediate and lasting effect on townscapes. Local authorities were required to enforce adequate sanitary conditions in their districts, and were empowered to make byelaws governing new development. Byelaw control covered such matters as the level, width and construction of new streets, and their drainage; the structure of foundations, walls, roofs and chimneys to give sound, reasonably fireproof and damp-proof buildings; minimum space around buildings for circulation of air and through-ventilation; water-supply, and the drainage of water-closets and other sanitary facilities; and closing of buildings that were unfit for habitation. Model byelaws adopted by most authorities prescribed detailed standards for development: carriage roads to have a minimum total width of 36 feet and for other roads 24 feet; yardspace at the rear of a dwelling to be of at least 150 square feet, with minimum depths of 10 to 25 feet for houses of heights under 15 feet to over 35 feet respectively; and so on.

The form of housing devised to meet byelaw standards, the 'tunnel-back', had a narrow frontage of some 15 feet and depth three times as much, thus giving minimum costs for road, paving, sewerage, water-supply reticulation, gas pipes and other services per foot frontage of dwelling accommodation, but at the expense of efficient daylighting of the rooms at the back. Such housing ranged in terraces along row after row of long, straight, parallel streets, lacking any relief in the shape of open spaces or playgrounds, and with the destruction of virtually every tree, hedge and blade of grass on building sites as the normal preparation for development. The triumph of sanitary reform was soured by the grim monotony of 'brick boxes with slate lids'. Little wonder that the 'genius' of local authorities of the time was referred to as 'an infinite capacity for laying drains'.

In the larger cities, mass-produced housing on a huge scale [28] all but smothered any lingering local vernacular styles for working-class housing. There were, nevertheless, exceptions to this generalization. Many towns which were expanding rapidly at this time, after the mid century, continued to express their 'sense of place' because it was as cheap to use local as imported materials; local builders

28. Sheffield: artisan housing, late nineteenth and early twentieth centuries.

therefore continued to build with them in their own traditional ways.

Reading is one of many examples that show a vigorous local building tradition, in this case of decorative blue-grey bricks alternating with red-browns or pale yellows to emphasize string-courses, quoins and window or door openings. Reading's nineteenth-century tradition is as outspoken in terraces for the working class or for artisans [29] as in more spacious semi-detached or detached residences in suburban districts. In the second half of the century an increasingly affluent middle class, anxious to devote its growing resources to new styles of building, as well as to opulent furniture and furnishings, greatly enlivened townscapes with an ingenious, if not always tasteful, assortment of designs, colours and textures, to be looked at in more detail later.

Increasing urban populations gave rise to needs for greater capacity in town halls, law courts, concert halls, museums, libraries, hospitals, prisons and other institutional buildings. The highly valued virtue of respectability (fortified by substantial grants from the state under the Church Building Act of 1811) also led to the building of many spacious and ornate churches : in fact no sizeable estate development was thought complete without one, and estate agents regarded their proximity as making residences even more 'desirable'. For this programme of buildings for public use, the styles prevailing at the opening of the century – revivalist Greek and revivalist Gothic – vied with each other, the former generally in the lead for the first thirty years or so.

Neo-classical forms, favoured for most public buildings, success-fully conveyed the sense of formality and dignity that might be expected of, say, the British Museum (1824–47), the Athenaeum (1827–30) or the Royal College of Surgeons (1835–6) in London, town halls in Birmingham and Leeds, and very many similar build-ings in Edinburgh, Glasgow and most provincial cities. But if neo-classicism succeeded in expressing the purpose and status of these kinds of building, it mixed somewhat uneasily with the business of a main-line railway: the noble porticoes of Huddersfield or Gosport

29. *Reading: Brighton Terrace, 1883: affectionate attention to detail in brickwork, from doorways to chimneys. One owner has since committed a breach of the visual peace by painting his entire elevation white, destroying the unity of the composition.*

railway stations seem to lose so much status as mere screens between a main town road and the messy, noisy interior of a station concourse. Picturesque and Castellated motifs, though at first more in evidence in country houses than in townscapes, became gradually more assertive in urban settings. An early application of Castellated to the building of prisons produced an exterior clothed with a seemly sense of severity and security that concealed the grim interior purpose, as at Reading Gaol (1842) and London's Holloway (1851).

Revivalist Gothic forged ahead with the publication, in 1836, of A. W. N. Pugin's *Contrasts*,[2] a strongly opinionated plea that architecture should once more become the means of expression of structure, and that decoration should emphasize the lines of construction, as had clearly been the case in the heyday of medieval church- and cathedral-building. The assertion, in the second paragraph of his thesis, 'that the great test of Architectural beauty is the fitness of the design to the purpose for which it is intended, and that the style of a building should so correspond with its use that the spectator may at once perceive the purpose for which it was erected' foreshadowed the concern with 'expression of function' that was to dominate architecture in the early twentieth century. Pugin's obsessively critical attitude towards neo-classical styles equated classicism with paganism. He even regarded St Peter's in Rome as a debasing departure from Christian notions of architecture, apparently disregarding the fact that early Christian churches traditionally echoed the form of a Roman basilica.

Pugin's *Contrasts*, subtitled 'a parallel between the noble edifices of the middle ages* and corresponding buildings of the present day; shewing the present decay of taste', hammered home the virtues of Gothic styles by juxtaposing examples of medieval buildings and their nineteenth-century counterparts, usually to the disadvantage of the latter. The appealing medieval Angel Inn at Grantham is compared with an Angel Inn at Oxford that seems to be a converted terrace house; Oxford's beautiful Christ's College gateway, adorned with processing academic dignitaries, contrasts with Smirke's

---

* The term 'middle ages' replaced the first edition's '15th century'.

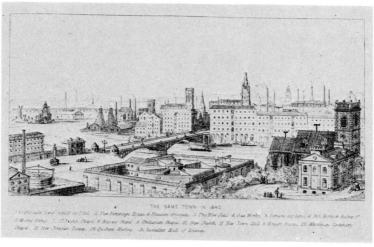

30. *Panoramas from Pugin's* Contrasts, *published 1836.*

classical gateway to King's College, The Strand, shown with disorderly protesters and passers-by. But the most telling townscape contrast is in the two plates* showing 'a Catholic town in 1440' and 'the same town in 1840' [30].

The one etching depicts a picturesque, compact town, serene and secure within a battlemented wall on the bank of a river, which is crossed by a bridge of many stone piers leading to the main town gate. Within the wall, delicate, soaring spires and towers of Gothic churches and guildhall, mingling with the steep-pitched roofs of tall, gabled houses make an appealing skyline; outside, the scene includes an abbey church, a smaller church, a market cross, and cottages straggling along lanes with spacious fields intervening.

The other etching is heavily critical of centuries of 'progress'. A new, broad, double-span iron bridge leads not to the town gate, for gate and walls have disappeared, but through a gap in a wall of five-storey mills into a coagulation of factories and pottery kilns with a skyline more of chimney-stacks than of church spires and towers. To add insult to injury, the top section of the tallest spire is broken off. Outside the former walls the Abbey is in ruin, the smaller church re-styled to suit the new, prosperous Palladian parsonage, and the market cross replaced by a classical monument, railed and surmounted by a globe. A large prison, a sewage works, a lunatic asylum and other developments have obliterated the former spacious fields.

Pugin's didactics were embodied in many buildings, great and small, that struck new notes in townscapes throughout the remainder of the century. His own masterpieces were largely confined to church architecture, but most of his feverish energy was devoted to the masterly detailing of Charles Barry's neo-Tudor Houses of Parliament. The variety and ingenuity of neo-Gothicism produced by Pugin's followers is readily apparent in a host of great creations: London's Law Courts, Public Record Office, Prudential Assurance Building and Midland Grand Hotel at St Pancras Station; town halls at Manchester, Congleton, Rochdale, Reading and Northampton [31] and the Theatre Royal at York are random examples. It

* Included in the second edition but not in the first.

31. Northampton: Town Hall (1864) in assertive Gothic; church at left rebuilt in 1680 after town fire: cupola, 1704.

32. London: Nos. 33-35 Eastcheap (1868) in effervescent Gothic, with a suggestion of French château at the top and quite unworthy modern adaptations at the ground floor; only one of five original doorcases survives (as left).

is no less apparent in innumerable smaller structures such as warehouses [32], office blocks, market buildings (Columbia Market, Bethnal Green), Institutes (York), working men's clubs, colleges, schools, hospitals, almshouses, fire stations and all manner of buildings, including houses, all over the country. The style was rather less convincing in expressing the function of a main-line railway station such as Bristol's Temple Meads.

But Gothic was by no means the prevailing style for this confident and inventive age. Classical designs derived from Greece or Rome, or via Renaissance versions, were still in favour for some town halls (Bolton, Birmingham, Leeds, Liverpool, Portsmouth) and other monumental structures (Free Trade Hall, Manchester, Walker Art Gallery, Liverpool). That they were also preferred for less ostentatious purposes is seen, for example, in Nonconformist churches and chapels whose congregations tended at first to equate the neo-Gothic form with Popery or High Anglicanism; many gracious classical façades still enrich small-scale unpretentious street pictures, as at Market Harborough or Basingstoke. By the mid-1880s, however, most Nonconformists, other than Quakers, had apparently been persuaded that Gothic was no less in good English tradition than were Doric, Ionic or Corinthian. Their 'new look' churches, with ornate patterns of coloured brickwork, tall, pointed arches and fine rose windows, soon became familiar features of many townscapes.

That designers of shop-fronts, too, were sensitive to style was earnestly stressed by Nathaniel Whittock in his *Illustrations of the Shop Fronts of London* (1840):[3]

If a grocer requires a front that will distinguish his shop from the draper or the ironmonger, any person but an architect would direct his attention to producing a design something in the Chinese or Indian style of decoration; but the very mention of the terms would distress a regular architect – to him sugar and tea would lose their flavour if they were not sold beneath a Grecian entablature, copied with great minuteness from a temple at Athens, dedicated to the worship of the Gods.

Wherever either [*sic*] of the five classic orders of architecture can be introduced with propriety, there is no person of the slightest taste but would wish to see them strictly copied from the most elegant examples of

Townscapes

Greece or Rome. Such should be selected for buildings or shops connected with learning or the arts, schools, the shops of booksellers, chemists, opticians, etc. The modern Italian or Palladian style, which admits of such a variety of ornament, is well adapted for tailors, dressmakers, haberdashers, drapers, and other light businesses connected with dress. Some first-rate drapers, who deal extensively with Indian goods, would be most properly distinguished by a splendid Indian front, selected from some of the gorgeous temples and pagodas that grace the banks of the Ganges.

Thanks to ... gentlemen that have studied those glorious ecclesiastical edifices called Gothic, the various styles of this species of architecture are now as well known and defined as the five classic orders, and under proper modifications the whole of them might be used for shop fronts with great advantage. Goldsmiths, watch and clock makers, book and print sellers, surgeons, chemists and druggists, might all use Gothic fronts with propriety; and there can be no doubt but shops for either of the above businesses, and many others, might be designed in the decorated English style, greatly superior in point of elegance to any that can be found in London, or any part of England at the present time.

The restless search for new styles for all kinds of structure went far beyond developing alternatives of Gothic for classical. An exuberance of ideas reflecting Egyptian, Byzantine, Italian palazzo, French château, German baronial, Dutch and Flemish Renaissance, 'Jacobethan', Japanese and all manner of motifs found expression in all manner of structures. Nothing was barred: Horlicks made malted milk in a factory with a medieval castellated exterior; colourful Moorish terracotta garnished with minarets was just the thing for St Paul's warehouse in Leeds [33]; but the same city's vigorous Yorkshire Penny Bank [34], or the remarkable Court of Justice in York, have less readily recognizable antecedents.

Style was not the only subject for innovation. Unprecedented uses, like those of railway stations and goods sheds, required not only unprecedented structures but also new materials for constructing and cladding them. Cast and wrought iron had been used decoratively in Georgian and Regency times for balconies, awnings, lantern brackets and the like [21, 22, 26], but its strength and versatility in terms of structure, as affirmed by the Coalbrookdale Bridge in 1779 and several other bridges soon afterwards, led to its increasing use for framed construction, for factories especially, as well as for sea-side

33. *Leeds: St Paul's warehouse (1878), Victorian Moorish, in brick and terracotta; missing minarets are being replaced.*

piers. It also proved useful for applied decoration. In conjunction with glass ('ferrovitreous' construction) cast iron also introduced vastly increased dimensions: the huge spans used for main-line railway stations (from the 1830s onwards) were little short of miraculous, and the designing of domes and the cult of conservatories, seen *in excelsis* in Decimus Burton's great Palm House at Kew Gardens, found its triumphant climax in the fabulous Crystal Palace (1851).

On a less spectacular scale, cast and, later, wrought iron brought felicitous touches of elegance to workaday townscapes. Shops occasionally appeared in the form of enclosed arcades; along street frontages many were reconstructed with slim columns, intricate brackets, delicate window-bars and elegant fascias and signs. The two unpretentious shops tucked away in Reading's Butter Market [35] have qualities which, if not apparently appreciated by their occupants, were not lost upon the Ministry Inspectors, whose assessment reads 'unusually attractive elaborately ornamented C.I. shopfronts of circular iron columns with applied vine ornament twisted round, and acanthus leaf capitals with a slightly Egyptian character'. Cast iron and glass were used to equally good effect for offices and

34. Leeds: Yorkshire Penny Bank (1894), ingenious mixture of motifs including Norman, Tudor and Italian palazzo.

35. *Reading: Butter Market: castiron shop-fronts for chemist and, formerly, gunsmith, dated 1857; the latter partly concealed by a clumsy modern fascia.*

36. *Market Harborough: Victorian mill, dominating small-scale townscape of seventeenth and twentieth centuries.*

warehouses, as seen in the text-book examples of Liverpool's Oriel Chambers, Macclesfield's Arighi Bianchi building and Glasgow's Jamaica Street warehouse. They were used even more decoratively in Lewis Sullivan's work in New York and Chicago, and no less pleasingly in Australian cities of the 1880s such as Bendigo and Melbourne.

Georgian and Regency architects had shown themselves able to keep abreast of the growing need of industry for factories, mills, warehouses and docks, and could match the size and form of the building to the number of operatives and the nature of the machines to be accommodated. Industrialization in nineteenth-century terms presented unprecedented problems. Immense and intricate machines for spinning, weaving and other processes required 'hands' by the several hundred, housed in buildings of unprecedented bulk which iron-framed, and later steel-framed, construction made possible. Such huge buildings began to dominate the townscapes of the day, and still do so, whether in small towns like Tadcaster or Horndean, over-shadowed by their breweries, or Market Harborough with its five-storey mill [36], or in the great manufacturing cities of the Midlands and North, such as Oldham, with their even bulkier and more over-bearing structures. Titus Salt's new 'Works', opened in 1853 in his model industrial town, Saltaire, was 550 feet long and six storeys high, with a 250-foot chimney, and housed 3,000 workers. Cecil Stewart[4] noted that it coincides in length and height with St Paul's Cathedral and covers a much greater area. Structures such as these continue to intimidate many a townscape at the present time.

The battle of styles between mainly neo-classical and mainly neo-Gothic was fought on the domestic front with equal zest as for public edifices, though not with such heavy architectural guns. Housing for the working classes produced, in general, a dreary townscape of long monotonous terraces along grids of long featureless streets. The watchwords for development were narrow frontage and great depth for each building, to gain maximum economy of land and road, sewer, drain and other costs per plot. Housing for the middle classes showed a more imaginative and adventurous approach to style and materials. The families of increasingly prosperous professional men, merchants and industrialists were prepared to expend various degrees of lavish-

37. *London: Woburn Walk (1825) by Thomas Cubitt; affectionately restored by LCC, but road surface in foreground not made good.*

ness on their houses as a means of demonstrating social status and good taste. Over the first half of the nineteenth century a high proportion of the housing, especially in large cities, was built speculatively and on quite a large scale by firms of builders following the precedent set by successful eighteenth-century developers like James Burton, builder of much of the Bedford Estate in Bloomsbury up to 1817. His achievement was far exceeded in skill and extent by Thomas Cubitt (1788–1855), who dominated building and the building industry for four decades.

Cubitt was the first speculative builder to operate with a large permanent staff comprising all trades; he built up several great 'works', well placed to serve particular developments in the locality, including brickworks, a large sawmill, smith's shop, masons' shops, plumbers', glaziers' and painters' shops, carpenters' and joiners' shops, and an extensive engineering works well equipped with expensive machinery.[5] He built solid, sound houses in prodigious numbers, principally terraced in complete streets or around squares, for the wealthy, the comfortable and the modest income brackets. Belgravia, Bloomsbury and Barnsbury are representative of his widespread operations in London; and one of his few urban ventures outside the capital city, the completion of Kemp Town, Brighton, is still a splendid piece of townscape. Most of Cubitt's work showed styles that reflected Georgian and Regency taste [37] and layouts that recognized the street or square as the unit of architectural design: each house, though internally independent, was externally subservient to the total composition.

This sense of subordination of the individual house to the street picture as a whole, so typical of the best of British townscapes of the great classical revival period, arose not only from the recognition that repetitive elements like houses made better townscapes collectively than individually. Terraces of narrow-frontage houses also achieved economies in land and construction and development costs. The tradition of long terraces of houses in long, straight streets thus continued into the late Victorian era, especially in areas where land values were high, as in what are now the 'inner rings' of large cities. But the tradition of restful visual continuity in the street scene was less highly valued. The desire to display social status and good taste was a rebellion against the well-mannered mass-produced uniformity of the classical tradition, and a substitution of individuality for collectivity. The street became a miscellany of adjacent houses. High Victorian Gothic residences sprouting all the favoured features – pointed arched windows, oriels, porches and the like – continued to be built, preferably on plots of four or six to the acre, aloof behind their laurels and shrubberies, and housing London City merchants in Ealing or fish-barons in Grimsby with fitting dignity. But such low-density development was too extravagant of land in town centres and tastes were, in any case, veering away from the excesses of 'true' Gothic.

The styles of domestic townscape representative of the last quarter of the nineteenth century are not easily defined because they were in many respects an exercise in novelty, a re-echoing of past styles. If one architect can be said to have exercised leadership among the many highly individualistic practitioners in rebellion against both classicism and neo-Gothicism, it was Richard Norman Shaw (1831–1912). The virtuosity and inventiveness shown in his enormous output of buildings over three and a half decades led Lutyens to regard him as 'our greatest architect since Wren, if not greater'; other architects equated his marked versatility with stylistic uncertainty.[6]

The label 'Shavian' sometimes ascribed to his work or that of his imitators is not very meaningful because he invented or adapted such a wide variety of styles. He brought about a 'Queen Anne' revival, seen in many of his town houses, but nowhere more felicitously than at his red-brick 'garden suburb' at Bedford Park, Chiswick (1876–1881), in which delicate detailing of several variations on Queen Anne architecture was brilliantly reproduced, though usually larger than life-size. He also drew freely upon the decorative motifs of the Franco-Flemish and Dutch Renaissance with such skill as to promote the popular 'Pont Street Dutch' vogue that still gives such gorgeous vivacity to so much of south-west London, especially Chelsea and Kensington. He revived Tudor half-timbering and plaster cladding or tile-hanging which, though effective in capable hands, was later demeaned by speculative builders to mere applied decoration. His Albert Hall Mansions set the fashion for elegant blocks of flats in London, and soon found an enthusiastic following. His last major public work, the Piccadilly Hotel, London (1905–8), is 'one of the best instances of the neo-Baroque mode which, along with other expressions, was current over the turn of the century. A series of grand, vigorously rusticated arches embodies shops at pavement level and, together with a shallow balconied tier immediately over, serves as a podium for an open Ionic colonnade, linking pavilions, behind which rises the main mass of the building'.[7]

Yet, in spite of so many vital and varied contributions, Shaw and his followers struck one jarring note which continued to reverberate over British townscapes. Although his individualistic designs could produce surprise and delight, he had little compunction in inserting an entirely new form of building into an existing group or terrace with arrogant disregard for prevailing styles or materials. For example, 196 Queen's Gate, London (1875), bright red, 'wholly of brick, rising from an asymmetrical ground floor in five twin-pilastered storeys to a scrolled, windowed and pedimented gable',[8] and greatly admired and widely imitated by contemporary architects, was thrust into a terrace of symmetrical 'Kensington Italianate' stucco residences [38]. This preoccupation with single buildings and disparagement of their neighbours, coming as it did from leaders of the architectural profession, made a break with the long-held tradition of terrace development in uninterrupted sequence; and the break remains unhealed.

Townscapes of the brief Edwardian era gained much from the output of two groups of architects whom Betjeman neatly named 'the silk-hatted' and 'the tweedy'. Although the groups tended to reflect the very pronounced class divisions of Edwardian society – the far too wealthy, the rich, and the comfortable middle class (the huge, abjectly poor working class obviously had no contact with architects) – they were not necessarily mutually exclusive. Doubtless they drew some inspiration from Norman Shaw (whose own wardrobe must have been as varied as his designs) but were far from lacking in ideas of their own. The silk-hatted, successful, persuasive, supremely self-confident practitioners usually preferred clients for whom nothing could be thought too good and whose purses, if not bottomless, were very well lined. Such clients, especially those in the private sector who liked their buildings to display their personal success, paid for, and

38. London: No. 196 Queen's Gate: Norman Shaw's lively but audaciously non-conforming 'new look'.

got, scintillating splendour. Classical styles were back in vogue: larger-than-life Renaissance designs, steel-framed and masked with Portland stone, displayed French, German or Italian, rather than English, accents. Gothic tastes were no longer much esteemed, although architectural inventiveness allowed free rein in design.

A few samples of the great wealth of Edwardiana could include Westminster's *Beaux Arts* Baroque Methodist Central Hall, William Whiteley's emporium and the florid terracotta Coburg Hotel in Bayswater, Oxford Street's grandiloquent Selfridge's Department Store, Bloomsbury's Imperial Hotel – 'a vicious mixture of Art Nouveau Gothic and Art Nouveau Tudor'[9] [39] in Southampton Row (since replaced after a fire by a far less likeable though doubtless much more profitable modern impersonal version) [40], and Piccadilly's quintessential Ritz Hotel. Outside London, Lan-

39. *London: Imperial Hotel, Bloomsbury: Edwardian design – 'a vicious mixture of Art Nouveau Gothic and Art Nouveau Tudor'.*

caster's Town Hall, Hull's Guildhall, Reading's Shire Hall, Reigate's Court House and Police Station and Caversham's Branch Library are random representatives of the numerous town halls, colleges, institutions, clubs and the like that still adorn and enliven almost any town anywhere in the country. These buildings, with their excellent materials and skilled craftsmanship, built by proud if sweated labour, stand solid and sure, seemingly confident of a long life and displaying an unabashed exuberance of decoration typical of the wealthy age that bred them. They rebuke the present wealthy but cost-conscious age that seems to have lost the art of producing buildings capable of inspiring much admiration or affection.

Betjeman's tweedy architects, who could sport a silk hat if their client was worthy enough, made less spectacular though equally memorable contributions to residential townscapes. The great majority of the 'lower orders of society' continued to live in dire

40. London: Imperial Hotel, Bloomsbury: modern version of the 1960s.

poverty in the crowded slums of large cities. The very well-intentioned efforts of industrialists like the Cadbury brothers and Lever brothers in building model villages for their employees inspired others, like Joseph Rowntree, James Reckitt and Arthur Markham, to do likewise; and the tweedy architects were instrumental in providing better house designs and site layouts which brought about a very gradual improvement in urban living.

Designers of outstanding ability, such as Raymond Unwin and Barry Parker, devised layouts with considerably lower densities than those prevailing in late Victorian times. Their detached, semi-detached and terraced housing, with private gardens at front and back, along grass-verged tree-planted streets or around planted squares and culs-de-sac, was given as pleasant a view and as good an orientation as possible. All residents could share the convenience of 'amenity' open spaces, children's play-spaces, local churches, shops and other buildings. All this development was drawn into a coherent residential unit with an identifiable sense of 'place', and was made virtually self-contained as regards day-to-day shopping and local social needs. Ebenezer Howard's first Garden City (Letchworth, 1903), designed and built by Unwin and Parker, showed a vast improvement on contemporary layouts of comparable houses.

The same team's Hampstead Garden Suburb (1906 onwards) was a memorable success; 240 acres of fields were transformed into a self-contained, consistently pleasing residential unit, comprising houses of a range of size and type to suit families of various income levels, and in a setting that soon became wonderfully sylvan despite its closeness to the built-up area of a great city. The new community had the advantage of a local centre with churches and a meeting place ('Institute') designed by Lutyens; the whole scheme provides, in the words of present-day residents, 'a very special kind of place and a picturesque, quiet, garden-like oasis in anonymous suburbia'.[10]

The work of Unwin and Parker, which may have been in part inspired by Norman Shaw's Bedford Park, undoubtedly raised standards of housing design and layout in both local authority and private building sectors. Together with a whole range of new designs from such inventive minds as Voysey, with his dislike of unnecessary ornamentation and feel for efficiency and comfort, Baillie Stewart, with his respect for local materials and methods of construction, and Lutyens, with his close regard for proportion and detail in neo-classical designs for residential, civic and commercial buildings, it helped to set the scene for much of the best of residential town-scapes of the twentieth century.

The tradition of Letchworth and Hampstead Garden Suburb was renewed in the delightful groupings of Welwyn Garden City (1920 onwards) and also, to some extent, in very extensive municipal enter-prises such as Wythenshawe, Speke and Becontree, although their very size and the standardized income-groups for which they were built militated against variety and personality. These achievements in turn begot imitations, some good but many inferior, from smaller municipalities and private speculative builders; collectively they led the way to some excellent townscapes in our post-1945 New Towns.

The impression may have been given that townscapes of the nineteenth century, indeed of any century, derived largely from the work of architects. This is not so. Good designs for houses, shops, offices and other buildings, prepared by architects for private clients, set a fashion and were often copied, although the quality and detailing suffered in the process, especially if they were mass-produced. A few leading architects contributed important set-pieces. But by far the greater share in making townscapes was taken by innumerable anonymous builders and developers, some from the public sector but mostly from private enterprise, churning out standard buildings by the dozen or by the hundred wherever sites were available.

Edwardian energy in embellishing townscapes flowed on during the five years from 1909 until the outbreak of the First World War. Ambitious plans, drawn up in the first few years of the new century and more remarkable for size and flamboyance than for originality of style, were brought to fruition or near-fruition. Typical of such developments in London were the comprehensive Kingsway/Aldwych redevelopment of a large slum area, the monumental addi-tions at either end of the Mall – the Victoria Memorial and Admiralty Arch – the County Hall (begun 1911, river-front part completed 1927) and many other civic and commercial buildings; and cities and towns all over the country could show similar acquisitions.

The era resounded with many other achievements of invention:

messages crossed the Atlantic by wireless signals; men flew in machines; but one particular achievement, destined to reverberate fairly gently during the pre-war period, but thereafter to crash into townscapes, made a quiet start. The evocative names that conjured it up – Napier, Sunbeam, Rolls-Royce, Lanchester, Vauxhall, Daimler – were of machines that all could admire but few could own and use. Horse-drawn carriages had been the chief means of transport within towns up till the 1840s. Most employees walked to their work in offices and factories; only principals and seniors could afford to travel daily by carriage or steam train. Concentration of economic activity in town centres and the extension of suburban rail services brought horse-drawn omnibuses and trams into use (the Reading Horse Tramway, for example, came into operation in 1879). These passenger services, adding greatly to the increasing volume of horse-drawn goods traffic on urban roads, caused considerable congestion. Horse-drawn buses and trams were gradually replaced from 1903 onwards by petrol-driven buses and steam, and later electric, trams; but personal transport by motor car, remaining as it did the prerogative of the rich, created no insurmountable road traffic problems until well into the inter-war period.

4: Twentieth-century components

During the inter-war years British cities and towns in general, and their central business districts in particular, lost more than they gained in terms of likeable and reassuring townscapes. The loss arose out of many factors. Constant growth of urban population necessitated more intensive use of central-area sites and greater floor-space in new buildings. Constant growth of vehicular traffic in towns, though still slight in comparison with developments in the 1950s and thereafter, brought problems of congestion and parking, and a growing crop of traffic signs. Street 'furniture' sprouted as profusely as traffic signs: lamp-posts, telephone boxes, post-boxes, direction signs and other objects added to the clutter in the environment, as did advertisement hoardings, neon signs and the rest. But probably the most significant loss arose from the inability of architects to find an architectural vernacular language for expressing the much larger and bulkier structures which framed construction made possible, and to handle the standardized components, new building materials and prefabricated units with which such structures were completed.[1]

British architects of the 1920s, with some notable exceptions, seemed to have run out of ideas in design. Although sure of their dislike of continual restatements of classical or Gothic or any other traditional styles, they seemed unsure of what to use in their stead. For important public buildings, and other major buildings such as headquarters of large concerns like banking houses and insurance companies, clients continued to demand – and architects generally relied upon – classical styles, though with more restrained decorative detail. Lutyens [41], Burnet and others still favoured the grand classical manner, and confidently clothed steel-framed or reinforced concrete carcases with stone-faced façades, regular fenestration,

41. London: Midland Bank, Poultry, by Lutyens, 1924; entrance emphasized with Tuscan columns; grand façade with upper floors united by tall arches.

accentuated entrances, columns, pilasters, mouldings, balconies, balustrades and other decorative features.

During the 1930s, also, important buildings were still appearing in classical forms, although all but shorn of ornament. The London Passenger Transport Building (1929) above St James's Park Station in London bore only sculptural ornament, by Epstein, Henry Moore, Eric Gill and others. The sparsely ornamented unlovable bulk of the Faraday building (1932) in London's Queen Victoria Street made a crude neighbour to the elegant College of Arms and a crude intrusion into a Thames skyline hitherto dominated by St Paul's Cathedral. The Royal Institute of British Architects headquarters (1934) in stately Portland Place was sparingly adorned, with a pair of detached columns topped by vague statues on the front elevation, and four figures in relief on the side elevation. The University of London Senate House (1939) in Bloomsbury, a massive pile faintly reminiscent of the Georgian style, was virtually bereft of embellishment. New buildings on sites previously built on were almost invariably given greater floorspace than had the buildings they replaced, and often appeared as oversized intruders in a hitherto reasonably harmonious environment and skyline. Yet the contrast they made was not quite so harsh as that made by the many bold and brash Victorian structures inflicted on predominantly Georgian surroundings a couple of generations earlier, or as some brutal intruders were to make in the 1960s.

The prewar 'Modern' style, if style it can be called, had emerged with no great clarity of definition from a series of movements, strands of thought and experiments, including Art Nouveau and 'Functionalism', which sought to make the forms and shapes of buildings expressions of the building materials and methods of construction in use at the opening of the century. Antoni Gaudi's Church of the Sagrada Familia and several blocks of apartments in Barcelona display his astonishing originality and skill in forming fantastic façades and shapes from stone, eccentrically decorated with ironwork and coloured tiles and glass. C. R. Macintosh's pioneer design for Glasgow School of Art (1899) had demonstrated that the appearance of a building could with advantage directly display its structural form. Auguste Perret's various works proved the suitability of reinforced concrete for both framing and panelling. Gropius and Mies van der

Rohe, with the benefit of inventive experience from the Bauhaus, introduced new forms of curtain walling for framed construction. Avant-garde 'modernists' continued to demand that every detail in the design of a building should be determined by its function, irrespective of appearance. Perret's declaration (possibly with tongue in cheek) that 'decoration always hides an error', and Corbusier's 'a house is a machine for living in', encouraged abandonment of traditional rules of elevational architecture.

Increasingly, architects of the late 1920s and early 1930s sought to arrive at a new vernacular language to express the modern age as clearly and confidently as the Georgians had expressed their own age two centuries previously. Their designs intended to show a building to be an expression of its function, to be made of what it was in fact made of, and to contain no more materials than were necessary for its purpose. Traditional qualities such as symmetry, balance, proportion and scale were seen less as the essence of good design than as logical response to user-requirements. Simplicity of form and appearance was the keynote. New buildings were of cuboid forms with flat roofs, flat façades, white walls, wide windows and minimal decoration. In competent hands, a block of flats [42], department store, hospital, library or any other building could be not only efficient and economic but clean-lined and visually satisfying and, above all, unassuming: noticeable but not clamouring for notice.

Increased use of concrete opened up new opportunities for moulding buildings as homogeneous structures in which visible surfaces could express the composition and purpose of the spaces enclosed. The greatest difficulty was the unattractive colour and texture of exposed surfaces. The natural grey of Portland cement, cold and depressing in appearance, became even less attractive after exposure to weather. Whereas brick and stone gained mellowness after years of exposure, concrete surfaces soon grew dirty, dark and stained, and also reflected even less light. Experiments with pigments to improve colouring were not rewarding at first, but of recent years progress has been made in the manufacture of concrete aggregate panels in pleasant shades and comparatively free from discoloration by the elements.

Additions or replacements in early post-1945 townscapes evinced greater concern for design as the science of achieving maximum usable

42. London: Palace Gate flats by Wells Coates, 1938; functional, well-mannered, using the minimum of building materials.

floor space and functional efficiency than as the art of achieving pleasing appearance. Modern methods of commerce called for increased floor area and units of larger size. A modern shopping centre comprised small shops, larger chain-stores and multiples and, later, even larger supermarkets, all giving priority of access to pedestrians at the front and to service vehicles at the side or rear. A new town-centre shopping group set out to serve shoppers by the thousand rather than the hundred, and spacious and unobstructed floor areas were therefore needed to develop self-service methods and to facilitate easy movement of shoppers with laden trolleys. Extensive areas for car-parking were also needed, at first or ground level and later in multi-decked form. The very successful prototypes for Coventry and Stevenage [43] set the precedent for this traffic-free yet traffic-accessible form of layout, and many equally successful redevelopments have been implemented in which the new 'pedestrian-only' forms merge easily into long-established shopping streets, as for

43. Stevenage: Town Centre (late 1950s): traffic-free shopping precinct.

example the Old George Mall in Salisbury or the new town-centre group in Basingstoke.

Modern office blocks in central-area locations were required to house not only hundreds of office workers at a time in well-lit accommodation, but also sophisticated filing systems and electronic computers. A large hotel or residential block in a central-area location was similarly required to provide the maximum floor area to reflect the value of its site.

Such large-scale buildings were usually of framed construction, and sometimes included modern mass-produced prefabricated units and panels. Vast expanses of transparent external walling exposed the structure to view: housings for lift-shafts and over-runs, ventilation shafts, water-tanks and mechanical and other services were treated as visual elements in their own right. Entrances to buildings were seldom emphasized and often unnecessarily difficult to locate; elevations were often graceless and monotonous [6]. Sir William (later Lord) Holford, speaking in 1964, deplored the effects of such 'non-design' on the built environment:

We all know office buildings, for example, where all the intelligence that went into their making was concentrated in the financial calculation of floor space, rental, and minimum cost; everything else such as external maintenance and cleaning, internal comfort and flexibility, good appearance, aspect, and recognition of their surroundings being organized just well enough to get by. Such buildings, if they do not ignore design altogether, regard it as an optional extra. An architect is employed with reluctance and – quite naturally in such circumstances – is grudged his 6 per cent.[2]

A very pronounced change in the form and silhouette of townscapes came after 1952, when the normal height-limit of 100 feet for buildings was relaxed and greater heights were permitted within plot–ratio limits, subject to structural safety and adequate means of fire-fighting. When the London County Council declared in 1956 that its policy for tall buildings would be to consider applications on their merits, London, and later other cities, began to sprout mini-skyscrapers. Their forms, as point blocks or slabs, emerged from such governing factors as light penetration, structural grid, airflow, housing of services, means of vertical access and logical size of usable spaces. Some were of considerable bulk because, their developers claimed, high

93

site-values necessitated full exploitation. The maximum usable floor space was achieved, but none spared for the extravagances that so delightfully capped many of the early American skyscrapers [44].

The ungainly, flat-topped tower blocks struck even harsher notes of discord in existing environments than had the brash giants of Victorian and Edwardian times. Many a fine building, such as a church or town hall, that had long presided visually over a particular area of a city or town was cut down to insignificance by overbearing newcomers. Bulky office blocks in Westminster diminished the dominance of the Abbey and the Houses of Parliament. The new Stock Exchange [45], glowering in the background, has snubbed the visual prestige hitherto vested in the Royal Exchange and the Old Lady of Threadneedle Street. St Paul's Cathedral stands embarrassed

45. *London: new Stock Exchange, belittling the Royal Exchange and Bank of* ▶ *England.*

44. *Chicago: the 'Magnificent Mile': skyscrapers capped by cupola, 'Gothic chapter house', spires, and other flights of fancy.*

though disdainful among gaunt, angular strangers [see cover picture].

This is not to say that tall buildings have no place in townscapes. On the contrary, throughout the centuries they have added richness and grandeur to urban skylines, and still do so. Chicago's huge but delicately detailed Civic Centre Building (1965), its brilliant twin-towered Marina City (1964) and many other powerful structures rise far above the ordinary to express greatness of character as well as of size. So does the slender slab of the United Nations Building in New York, though it unfortunately produced many poor imitations. So also do the Commercial Union Assurance office in London's Leadenhall Street, Thorn House in St Martin's Lane [46], New Zealand House in the Haymarket, Castrol House in Marylebone Road, and the three great towers at the Barbican. But not many others achieve this. What is vital to townscapes and town planning is that tall buildings should be located so as not to impair good views and historic skylines, or overload traffic routes in the vicinity.

An unappealing aspect of modern architecture appeared during the 1960s, when brutally coarse and alien structures were thrust into townscapes with apparently no regard for the surroundings in which they were to be set. Their forms seem to have been dreamt up *in vacuo*, the only consideration that may have been given to townscape being that neighbouring buildings should follow their enlightened example on redevelopment. Their begetters, having repudiated traditional rules of elevational architecture, embarked upon what can only be called non-styles. These embraced eccentricity and discord, delighted in coarse and undressed surfaces (especially concrete simulating the grain of timber shuttering), crudely exposed reinforced-concrete beams and shafts, ducts and housings for services, lumpish pillars, clumsy handrails, heavily framed external covered walkways and vast, stark concourses. The appearance of such buildings became more unsavoury as stains and blotches resulted from weathering.

The South Bank of London (the Hayward Gallery [47] in particular) and the forbidding Tricorn Shopping Centre at Portsmouth are typical of this crudely assertive architecture. Hardly less crude, though with cleaner and more colourful surfaces, is the weighty assemblage of units, including a 300-foot tower, bearing down on an exceptionally

46. *London: Thorn House (1954), St Martin's Lane: a tall, well-detailed modern office block.*

47. *London: Hayward Gallery; massive investment of concrete producing startling, ungracious townscape.*

attractive site that separates the urban grace of Knightsbridge from the rural grace of Hyde Park. The Knightsbridge Barracks affords an inelegant home for the most elegant and colourful unit of the British Army. An eminent architect, while praising its architecture as 'distinguished, personal and exuberant', condemned its siting as 'a disaster...the architectural gain is townscape loss.'[3] His criticism exemplifies the strange lack of consideration which even leaders of the architectural profession can show for the siting of new buildings in well-established townscapes.

Although the pendulum of architectural style seems to have swung away from the ugly and assertive, it shows few signs as yet of moving towards the elegant or even the pleasing. Architecture, as already noted, can be equated with fine art only in rare instances as, for example, in the design of a cathedral or other building of monumental character. It is an art that does not demand recognition of individualistic expression from the practitioner. The urban architecture normally appreciated by the townsman is that which does not compel him to look at it: the kind that forms a quiet, even slightly self-

A The rchitect

JANUARY 1972

"I am the heir to eight centuries

of architectural experience.

I have had a five-year course

at a School of Architecture.

I have passed the Final Examination

of the Royal Institute of British Architects.

And when it comes to an architectural elevation

suitable for a city street this is the

best I can do."

48. Cover of the Architect, *January 1972.*

effacing, background to everyday life, not clamouring for attention or announcing a marvel of achievement, content, like good Georgian townscape, to be seen as if it had always been there and really belonged there. But with few exceptions, modern buildings continue to be unprepossessing in appearance and poor in external quality; and their greatest critics are architects themselves. The cover of the *Architect* for January 1972 bore a sad confession [48].

To the layman, modern buildings are indeed too often unsatisfying, both in themselves and as components of modern townscapes. Individually they too often reflect private greed and public meanness. They are made as large as the planning authority will permit, and they wring every bit of exploitable value from every square foot of site area. Their form is flat-faced, flat-topped and free of attempt at embellishment [6]. Their finish is often poor; they often weather badly; and the standard of finish adopted for the front elevation is often denied to elevations which, though not intended to be seen, *are* seen – for example, the rear approach to a 'pedestrian' shopping centre from a car park.

Collectively, as additions or replacements to townscapes, modern buildings are too often alien to, and destructive of, urban quality and character. Developers show a remarkable degree of indifference to continuity in townscapes: it is as if they see a building site as a blank sheet on the drawing board. Whilst it is fair to say that the interior of a building belongs to the client and must reflect his requirements, it is no less fair to say that the exterior 'belongs' to the town and will have to be looked at by people for generations to come. To a surprising extent, city and town councils have allowed themselves to be persuaded that proposed buildings deserve planning consent as satisfactory components of townscape when, in fact, they detract violently from it. The arrogance with which some architects argue their cases, and their disregard for any expression of opinion by non-architects, has lost them much of the respect that laymen usually accord to professional men. J. M. Richards, addressing fellow-architects, pulled no punches:

I'm not speaking only of the architects who show themselves unable to use materials that don't look shabby a few years later, or who lack the other practical skills they ought to command as a matter of course. I'm speaking even more about architects whose buildings are destructive to their surroundings, including successful architects, who ought to know better, who cannot resist important commissions when they know perfectly well that what they are building, however skilfully they may design it, ought not to be where it is on environmental grounds; who site high buildings where they damage the whole landscape to flatter a client's self-esteem, or who connive at creating isolated monuments that break up existing comprehensive layouts.[4]

Architecture is not the only subject for praise and criticism in townscapes. Engineers responsible for public utility services and traffic control, and local authorities and other public and private organizations discharging their various duties, have contributed to the urban scene a multifarious mass of objects collectively called 'street furniture'. Some such objects have claimed a place in streets over many centuries as, for example, the statues, triumphal arches, obelisks and other embellishments of ancient Egypt, Greece and Rome.

Probably the oldest utilitarian item is the fountain or well, where citizens congregated not only to collect the daily water supply but to exchange news and gossip. Although by Renaissance times the fountain had become a decorative feature, it continued to exist long after water-supply had been piped to houses in Victorian times. Indeed, since its foundation in 1859, the Metropolitan Drinking Fountain and Cattle Trough Association has erected at strategic points in streets and squares more than 2,800 drinking fountains for 'human beings' (originally to reduce consumption of cheap gin). The 4,600 troughs which they erected from motives of kindness to horses and dogs have long outlived their purpose, and most have been removed, though some remain to house floral decorations. (In their day, horse troughs must have been as much a cause of congestion to horse-drawn traffic in urban streets as are petrol stations to motor traffic nowadays.)

A count of items of street furniture in a distance of, say, a hundred yards in any main street will disclose the extent to which the problem has grown: there could be lamp-posts, traffic lights, traffic-control and directional signs, telegraph poles and wires, pillar-boxes, stamp machines, telephone boxes, police boxes, transformer boxes, fire hydrants, rubbish-bins, grit-boxes, bus stops and shelters, benches, bollards, railings, public lavatories, statues and other sculptures, trees, shrubs, flower-boxes, and yet other items.

Much of the visual confusion arises from the fact that this increasing clutter of objects is provided by a multiplicity of local authorities, statutory undertakers and public and private organizations. Each body has performed its individual function with efficiency and good intention and has designed visible items of equipment to look like what they are. But they seem to have paid little heed to the cumulative effect of their contributions to the scene as a whole. The growth of vehicular traffic in towns has produced probably the richest crop of items: streets now sprout signs: no left turn; no right turn; no entry;

49. Aylesbury: market square with a bumper crop of street furniture. This includes: statues – Disraeli commending a footwear shop and Hampden defying the County Hall; 13 visible posts (excluding lamp-posts) bearing traffic lights and assorted signs; 2 war memorials, one concealed by a 'no entry' sign, the other behind the Clock Tower and accompanied by a cattle trough, telephone box and corrugated-iron shed; railings, post-and-chain boundary, seats, flower-pot, traffic-light control box, and so on. Compared with market places in some other towns, Aylesbury's is relatively uncluttered.

no parking; no waiting; no loading; no speed limit; 70, 50, 40 or 30 miles an hour. There are the daubs of single and double yellow lines, pedestrian crossings and beacons, parking meters, television camera 'eyes', and so on. All these and more seem to thrive and increase on a diet of petrol and oil, and each one seems to want a pole or post of its own. Lack of coordination in all kinds of 'official' furniture is most in evidence at street intersections, where traffic lights, traffic signs, directional signs, telephone boxes, pillar-boxes and other items all claim a place [49].

Street furniture comprises broadly utilitarian and broadly decorative items. Chief among the utilitarian is street lighting, which has not only to give the degree of night illumination appropriate to the width and purpose of particular streets and places, but also to fit sympathetically into the daytime surroundings. The size and height of lamp standards varies with street widths and functions: heights of 30–40 feet are recommended for 'A' roads, to provide adequate illumination for drivers; 16 feet is the recommended height for 'B' roads; for minor roads and pedestrian ways, however, heights can be about 13–15 feet, related to the heights of people and their houses and front doors and garden gates.[5]

Lamp standards and other forms of illumination may be of visual benefit to townscapes in two ways: either as a conscious component of urban design, or as a component made as unnoticeable as possible. The 'noticeable' approach is seen to best advantage in formal, even monumental, settings: the beautifully decorative craftsmanship of lamps and standards greatly enhances the elegance of London's Mall, Constitution Hill and Embankment [70], as the short cast-iron George IV columns and fine lanterns of curved glass do in Regent's Park. Memorable also are those in Dublin's streets and squares [22] and in most Spanish cities, and those in the Place de l'Opéra, Paris, which so strongly accentuate the formal beauty of the square at night. Equally well-mannered, though less assertive, are the small Victorian gas-lamp standards [37], converted to electricity and lining streets and squares in Chelsea, Kensington and similar quiet residential areas of eighteenth- and nineteenth-century date. (The kind of lamp which Richard le Gallienne described: 'Leaping a light on either hand, the iron lilies of the Strand'.) Replacement of such equipment by mass-produced concrete standards has removed an important component of some older urban areas; and only forceful protests from residents have prevented further 'improvements' in others.

The 'unnoticeable' approach is more utilitarian. It accepts the illumination engineer's recommendations for functional distribution of the sources of light and implements them with apparatus as inconspicuous and streamlined as possible [3, 21, 27, 31, 42], so that, once installed, hardly one person in a hundred notices its presence by day. Lighting equipment of this type achieves the greatest visual success by drawing the least attention to its existence. Lamp standards need to be slim and of a colour and texture sympathetic to the environment for which they are designed. Cast-iron standards could be delicately moulded and formed as one complete unit; but they had to be painted at regular intervals. Concrete standards need no maintenance; hence the enthusiastic adoption by parsimonious borough and district councils of rough, grey concrete standards in the late 1930s and post-war period. Mass-production techniques led to the manufacture of the standards by one group of firms and the lanterns by another; the marriage between standard and lantern was then conscientiously performed by the borough engineer at the minimum of cost to ratepayers.

The various forms of lamp standard and lantern, and the disconcerting changes in strength and colour encountered at the boundaries between local authority areas, have attracted so much criticism and ridicule in recent years as to cause councils not only to seek more sympathetic designs for equipment, but also to coordinate colours and reject those which are uncomplimentary to the human complexion. Better results have been achieved by the use of new sources of light (notably the colour-corrected mercury light) in old lanterns on cast-iron columns [23, 37] as well as with modern equipment. Streets are also being efficiently illuminated by lamps attached to brackets on buildings [19] rather than to posts on the pavements. Stevenage, Crawley and Harlow New Towns set an attractive precedent in this respect, but municipal councils are often discouraged by the difficulty of gaining consent from all building owners concerned.

Bus stops, shelters, telephone boxes, police boxes, sales kiosks

50. Dublin: O'Connell Street, the city's broad main street, with many fine buildings, some debased by crude advertisements; public lavatories sited on an inaccessible island and flanked by tatty dustbins.

and similar items are also distributed without much regard for visual effect in the street as a whole. A measure of coordination and combination is certainly possible : bus shelters of framed steel or reinforced concrete, walled and roofed with glass and other light-weight panels, might be combined with telephone boxes, litter-bins and, possibly, sales kiosks. As with street lighting, it is possible to treat bus and other shelters as positive decorative elements in the street – as was successfully done in Victorian and Edwardian seaside towns and spas ; but in busy urban streets they are best treated as noticeable but visually minor elements. Public conveniences should also be located where most people congregate and be made readily recognizable and accessible, though not visually dominant. An excellent siting was achieved in Stevenage New Town shopping centre. The monumental Victorian public lavatories, often sited in the middle of crossroads, are even more unsuitably placed in modern traffic conditions than they were in the days of horse-drawn traffic [50].

Townscapes

The 'wirescape' of light and power cables and telephone lines, a visually messy and unfortunate feature of modern townscapes, creates both a monotonous march of ugly posts along footways and a drab linear pattern in the space above. Although much wire has been placed underground in densely populated urban areas, it persists noticeably in smaller towns and villages. Removal of overhead cables in towns of historic and architectural interest, such as Lavenham, has brought impressive visual improvement to fine medieval and other townscapes, though much has still to be done to improve the everyday scene elsewhere.

The use of railings, low walls, bollards and other forms of barrier in towns is increasing with the need to define and separate areas and routes for different purposes. In particular, they segregate routes of movement for pedestrians and vehicles, and discourage pedestrians from crossing streets at places where vehicular traffic is at its most dense. The bollard, in cast iron, steel, stone, or concrete and chippings, gives firm visual definition to urban spaces of all kinds; it proclaims an authoritative 'no entry' to vehicles, but a safe passage for pedestrians. Barriers of any kind benefit from design in sympathy with surrounding buildings and from being built of materials typical of the locality.

Among the decorative kinds of street furniture, sculpture has the deepest roots in townscape, dating from even earlier than the Greek *agora* and Roman *forum*. Its origin in British townscapes is associated with late medieval and early Renaissance practice in Italy, and thence through the various adaptations of Renaissance ideas in the northern Europe of the seventeenth and eighteenth centuries. 'Street' sculpture takes broadly two forms: the representational, and the symbolic or abstract. Representational sculpture includes statues of monarchs, heroes, statesmen, benefactors and others, usually designed and placed so as to be in scale with their settings and seen to best advantage [16]. Monumental versions, such as London's Nelson's Column, Duke of York column and Roosevelt Memorial, preside nobly over their surroundings, as do the splendid Arc de Triomphe and Colonne Vendôme in Paris. As most statues of less than monumental proportions are meant to be approached and looked at by pedestrians, they are unhappily located if space is not available for people to pause by them. Their relocation, replacement or abandonment must also be considered when changes are being made to the urban fabric in the locality, when buildings take on different uses or are replaced in different size and shape, and when roads are converted to pedestrian ways (or vice versa) or crossroads redesigned as roundabouts.

Such changes can give rise to absurdities: a Victorian statesman in toga and laurel wreath who originally struck a noble attitude at a street junction may now appear to be directing traffic at a roundabout; a social reformer in frock-coat and stovepipe hat, originally gazing approvingly towards an orphanage, may now be facing a discothèque or amusement arcade. Nor do statues retain their relevance forever. Monuments to dictators in totalitarian countries are often changed in rapid succession. Queen Victoria now presides over fewer civic squares in former colonial cities and towns, though she lingers in urban settings in Britain.

Symbolic or abstract sculptures are intended to decorate and add distinction to the physical environment. They can help to 'inhabit' streets and places and give them a special identity. Their placing may be formal, as in the Renaissance 'set-piece' design, or informal,

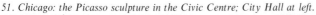
51. Chicago: the Picasso sculpture in the Civic Centre; City Hall at left.

in the manner so clearly described by Camillo Sitte in his reference to children's snowmen.*

A piece of sculpture that brought an immediate sense of identity, controversy and fun to an important urban setting is the Chicago Civic Centre sculpture, commissioned from Picasso in 1964 by the City Fathers.† Erected by architects and engineers in 1967, this gigantic work [51], 60 feet in height, is made of steel with profiles and surfaces in sheet metal of rich rust-red texture and iron rods enclosing the spaces between them; it is overshadowed by huge multi-storey slabs and towers. The piece fascinates and demands attention. People come to gaze at it, photograph it, ask what it is, discuss it, admire it, analyse it, criticize it: to show, in fact, any reaction except apathy.

Water in the urban scene has a strongly attractive quality for visitors or passers-by, young and old alike. Especially fascinating is the fountain, with its lively play of sparkling light and the glistening vitality it brings to wet sculpture. The more restful quality of pools and basins tends to draw people together, in shopping centres for example, where adults pause to gossip while their youngsters sail match-box or paper boats. Neglect of maintenance, however, can easily transform these pleasurable features into rubbish-laden eyesores.

Among the features all but lost from mature townscapes over the years is the rich variety of surfaces over which people could walk or ride. 'Floorscape' or 'footscape', as these have come to be called, has attracted increased interest in recent times since the 'pedestrian precinct' came back into vogue. Once it became possible to free particular areas within the urban framework from the motor vehicle and its accompanying dirt, oil, tyre-marks and other unpleasantness, the urban 'floor' could be modelled with something like the variety that people like to see in the floors of buildings. The ancient art of paving came into its own again. Early Renaissance architect–planners had shown their skills in making a formal composition of buildings and spaces into a powerful unity with

* See above, p. 29.
† The old man is said to have deflated the commissioning deputation with the question: 'Where is Chicago?'

patterns of paving that echoed and emphasized the main framework of the composition and guided the eye to decorative architectural features, to entrances to buildings and to exits from spaces. Rome's Piazza di San Petro and Venice's Piazza San Marco are two of the many splendid formal compositions that set a pattern of elegance for centuries to come. Medieval towns achieved little in the way of efficiency or formal decorative quality in paved urban surfaces, even though pavage taxes were being levied six centuries ago. Nevertheless, the variety in colour and texture of surfaces, reflecting the local materials used for the towns' buildings, contributed much to their informal interest and character. Ludlow, in common with many other long-established towns, lost much of its visual interest a couple of decades ago when its characteristic cobbled streets were covered with smooth asphalt to please motorists; only a few sloping cobbled verges remain as evidence of former textures.

Materials that produced flat and reasonably smooth surfaces, such as flagstones [19], paving slabs and tiles, granite setts [9, 37] and brick-on-edge, were used conventionally to indicate surfaces for people to walk on; whilst materials producing uneven or uncomfortable surfaces, such as cobbles or flints [43], acted as a deterrent to movement across them. These conventions are still relevant today. In particular, an area of cobbles conveys the clear message to pedestrians and drivers alike: 'Keep off!' Floorscape can convey other messages as, for example, in Cumbernauld and other new towns, where one tiled pattern on footpaths indicates the routes from residential areas to the local shopping centre or town centre, while another pattern shows the routes to schools and helps children find their way. Variations in pattern can visually reduce the extent of a broad space, such as a town square, by subdividing it into different local uses: there may be surfaces to denote through-routes for walkers, to steer walkers away from flower-tubs and troughs [59], to place benches on, to allow penetration of rainwater to tree-roots, and so on.

Study of ground-surfaces in old towns – cobbles in districts plentiful in flint, pebbles in a sea-port, stone setts in a northern market town, flagstones in a cathedral close, paving around a fountain – can suggest means for perpetuating and enriching the character and

109

liveliness which age and maturity have moulded. Above all, the borough engineer must be restrained from reducing all surfaces to the smooth tarmacadam or asphalt which motorists and pedestrians appreciate. Clearly these smooth surfaces make easy routes of travel for vehicles and walkers; but routes of travel do not account for all unbuilt urban space. Floorspace of various patterns helps to relate individual buildings and spaces to each other and to the immediate locality; whereas buildings that arise from a homogeneous surface of asphalt, tarmac or concrete remain separate entities with less of a sense of unity and belonging. Large areas of granite setts still lie just beneath the tarmac in many a town, and could easily be brought to light once more.

The borough engineer must also ensure that, where surfaces of brick, setts, flagstones or other characteristic material are disturbed by the digging of trenches for services, the disturbance is made good not by asphalt – as is so often the case [3, 14, 37] – but with the original material. He can also use his influence in another respect. Cities and towns in the industrial North are especially rich in stone and other floorscape materials. Yet when redevelopment or rehabilitation is taking place – as for example a 'General Improvement Area' operation – people sometimes ask for modern materials such as concrete slabs or tiles which they regard as 'fashionable'. To follow alleged 'fashion' at the expense of rejecting a strong local character and tradition brings no visual gain, but probably a visual irritant, to the locality.

Striking changes in townscape have come from cleaning prominent buildings. The former Lord Mayor of London who commemorated his term of office by initiating the cleaning of St Paul's Cathedral set a precedent for the whole country. The National Gallery, the Law Courts, the Albert Hall, the Natural History Museum in Kensington and government offices in Whitehall are among the many London buildings that have emerged in pristine splendour, sometimes reproaching their neighbours [52]. Cleaning does not necessarily enhance appearance, however. Years of weathering can accentuate relief in façades and give mellowness, to brickwork especially, though concrete surfaces do not often improve over time. Nor does cleaning solve the problem of deterioration. The

52. London: the gleaming Foreign Office puts to shame the dirty knights of Middlesex Guildhall.

water used in the process combines with the sulphur dioxide present in layers of soot to form sulphuric acid, which is destructive of stone; and removal of grime exposes cracks and can lead to further flaking.

Even if townscapes benefit from sympathetic (and clean) architecture, well-controlled street furniture and characteristic floorscape, they may still be disfigured by crude or excessively numerous advertisements. Signs of all kinds and sizes, from small plaques and panels to vast hoardings, clutter shopping streets and create distractions for drivers. The need for advertising is not in question, but its methods are. When every shop in a street clamours visually for attention, the effectiveness of advertisement for the individual shop is inevitably weakened.

It is unfortunate, too, that most multiple stores and large retailers use their premises as advertisements in themselves by applying standard 'house rules' for façades, fascias and lettering, without regard to geographical location or to the scale, proportion and style of their neighbours. The same shop-front is imposed in Oxford Street,

111

London, as in the high street of Oxford, or of a cathedral city, county town or suburb. Rigid adherence to this practice on the part of large concerns with the necessary influence to get their own way has caused townscapes to lose much of their distinctive identity. To criticize this practice is not to advocate medieval Marks and Spencers or Tudor Tescos: it is to advocate greater respect for local building materials and textures, and for particular characteristics of scale, vertical emphasis, plot-frontage width and similar local circumstances, so that redevelopments can be modern, but still mannerly, neighbours.

Standards of advertisements regarded as acceptable for some parts of a city or town centre may be less so for other parts. Piccadilly Circus, or Times Square in New York, or almost anywhere in the central areas of Tokyo, Los Angeles, San Francisco or any great city, are transformed by night into magical scenes of brashly colourful, vivacious wonderland. By daylight, the same places in most cities – Piccadilly Circus especially – show building façades of sordid shabbiness. Regent Street, by contrast, still possessing a measure of formal grandeur (though not the one Nash gave it), gains more from formal types of advertising confined to fascia-level only; and it assumes an exceptional gaiety at Christmas time, when decorations span the street high above the traffic and draw shoppers and spectators in large numbers.

Increasingly, the jarring effects of advertisement hoardings and neon signs are giving place to a more creative and well-mannered approach, in which advertising takes its place as a planned item of street furniture. Shops are being relieved of the clutter of signs and plates and boards and, instead, are gaining more telling attraction with fewer and more effective messages. High-level signs, too, are becoming less dominating and disfiguring. (Scandinavian countries have done much to raise standards.) The Place de l'Opéra, Paris, affords an inspiring example with its neon signs, which blend quietly but incisively with the admirably formal street-lighting to which reference was made earlier.

The cardinal cause of deterioration in twentieth-century town-scapes is the one that has emerged several times already in this book: the huge increase of motor traffic on urban roads. The boon of personal mobility exacts its price from the environment in congestion, pollution, noise, and damage to buildings, as well as from pedestrians and drivers in a fearsomely increased accident-rate. City and town engineers have tried in vain to keep abreast of growing demands for space to accommodate vehicles, in motion or at rest. The action they could take with the resources available was no more than palliative. Widening carriageways and junctions by straightening building lines, shaving off corners and removing obstacles such as fountains or market crosses brought temporary improvements in speed and flow of traffic, but at the cost of depriving the townscape of features that contributed to character and sense of enclosure. The greater the space made available, the more the vehicles that came to occupy it and the greater the congestion in central areas where additional space could not be provided at other than prohibitive cost.

It became evident to the government some years ago that construction of more roads and parking space to meet unrestrained demand could lead not only to greater congestion and danger, but also to an unacceptable amount of mutilation of urban fabric of high architectural, and possibly historic, quality. Hence the Buchanan Report (*Traffic in Towns*), which called for a hierarchy of urban roads, environmental areas and improved traffic management, and concluded that acceptable environmental standards could in some cases be attained only by imposing a measure of restraint on free access of vehicles to town centres.

Buchanan's design principles, which expose the need for unprecedented investment in road improvement and the rearrangement of patterns of circulation, would if implemented bring significant changes in townscapes, notably in new forms of 'traffic architecture'. Beneficial though such changes might be in terms of easier flow of traffic, their implementation could lead to other difficulties. In their determination to secure separate routes of travel for 'through' and 'local' traffic, the authorities may fail to recognize that local traffic can bring nearly as much environmental nuisance as 'through' traffic: as, for example, the heavy lorries which penetrate back streets in central areas to deliver or collect goods and materials from shops, warehouses and factories. Moreover the splitting of a town into a series of small environmental areas separated from each other by distributor roads of realistic width, whether achieved by converting existing roads into distributors or constructing new roads, is itself very damaging to the environment. Also, the progress of travel for pedestrians or cyclists between one environmental area and another may prove quite hazardous.[6]

Although the Buchanan design principles have been shown to be fairly applicable to small towns, such as Chichester or Canterbury or Basingstoke, they present formidable problems of implementation in large cities in the two respects just mentioned. More efficient distributors could enable a greater volume of 'local' traffic to enter environmental areas; and the act of constructing such distributors can result in the devastation of great swathes of urban fabric along their routes – as vividly demonstrated in recent years in London, Birmingham and elsewhere. In these respects, the outcome of colossal expenditure on traffic improvement could well be more loss than gain to townscapes.

The impact of the motor vehicle on townscapes is starkly in evidence in the layout of modern urban roads, especially in residential areas. For the past three decades, the guidance offered to highway engineers in two Ministry manuals – *Design and Layout of Roads in Built-up Areas* (1946) and *Roads in Urban Areas* (1966) – has resulted in a standardized environment almost as inflexible as that produced by the Public Health Act, 1875. Recommended traffic 'lanes', road curves, sight-lines and so on, related to various speeds of traffic, have been assiduously implemented. The problems are crystallized in the opening paragraph of the 1966 manual, which states that 'urban roads should be designed to be safe and to permit free flow of traffic at reasonable speed'.

Safety and free flow for pedestrians and drivers alike, each an admirable aim, are incompatible. Safety for drivers requires carriageways wide enough to let vehicles pass or overtake, smooth curves to give the necessary visibility without impeding progress at various speeds, adequate splays at road junctions for safe entry to other roads, adequate weaving length at roundabouts, and so on.

But safety can be dearly bought at the price of catering for a wide range of contingencies. Free flow of vehicles at increasing ranges of speed brings increasing danger to pedestrians; and the higher the speed and the freer the flow, the greater the areas of land needed to serve the vehicle. Recommended lane-widths varying from 12 feet on primary distributors to 9 feet on residential roads result in a carriageway-width of 18 feet for the most minor of residential roads. Highway engineers adopt this minimum width, but often increase it to allow sufficient space for large vehicles such as removal pantechnicons, oil service-tankers or refuse-collection carts to pass each other. Turning circles in culs-de-sac are given radii large enough for a refuse cart to turn without backing or manoeuvring. Similarly, footpaths in residential areas are given a 6-foot width to allow mothers with prams to pass each other.

These 'safety margins' envisage confrontations which occur very infrequently and may never occur at all. Large vehicles are infrequent visitors which might occasionally cause momentary inconvenience to a few drivers; mothers with prams do not follow a collision course and could easily negotiate an encounter on a narrower footway. Adoption of these margins has created the large, mostly empty and desolate spaces typical of the modern residential estate which were effectively described in an article in the *Architectural Review* of October 1973 entitled 'SLOAP' (Spaces Left Over After Planning).[7] An alternative was argued:

> The dominance of the car is largely responsible for the typical modern housing estate becoming a sophisticated form of visual, environmental and, in the private sphere, financial cruelty: wasteful of land, devoid of identity, and bereft of townscape.
>
> But the price of re-creating townscape and of liberating modern housing from the strait-jacket into which it has been forced is no more than the subjecting of the road vehicle to the human and domestic scale *when it is in the residential area to which that scale applies.*
>
> Private cars only need to be given the right of access, not of an uninterrupted flow from starting point to destination. In selected areas, large vehicles – including fire engines and furniture vans – can be treated as the exceptions they are rather than as the norm, and space provided for occasional access only. This space need be no more than 16 feet wide in total from house front to house front to accommodate realistic vehicle and pedestrian access needs.

Relaxation of these margins would not only help designers to re-introduce the sense of place and of enclosure that characterizes mature townscapes intended originally for pedestrians. It would also make possible higher densities of development resulting from savings in road-space.

5 : Conservation of the urban environment

If a healthy complexion and good looks in a person are normally signs of a sound physical constitution and a healthy way of life, much the same may be said of a town. A good-looking townscape is the product of a host of factors. These include: a workable structure of compatible land-use groupings, attractive layout and pride in the craftsmanship of buildings old and new, suitable densities of development, efficient public utility services, convenient routes for vehicles and pedestrians, open space in appropriate amounts and locations, clearly defined urban–rural boundaries, space for expansion and, above all, a viable economy. Seen in these terms, most of our towns have neither a healthy complexion nor good looks. Over the centuries their inhabitants have abused them by making them serve purposes for which their structure was unfit, letting them develop heart strain and put on weight in the wrong places, clotting their circulation with excessive traffic flow in narrow streets, damaging their fabric by neglecting to maintain it in good working order, and making unjustified demolitions and unworthy replacements.

Even if it were possible to agree how to stem the flow or repair the consequences of such acts and omissions, the task is probably beyond the capacity of the present generation and the next. The capital invested in buildings and public utility services in a town as a whole is seldom capable of rapid and profitable replacement, although very substantial profits have been, are being, and will be made by demolishing individual buildings or groups on commercially attractive sites in selected towns and redeveloping at much higher densities.

The restoration of good urban health calls for continuous and coordinated treatment in three main respects : first, keeping the body of the town intact and maintaining its health to facilitate everyday economic and social activity ; second, applying surgery to improve circulation and remove diseased parts ; and third, breathing new life into outworn areas or creating new environments on old or new sites. These three kinds of treatment approximately represent : conservation; central-area renewal; and rehabilitation, redevelopment and extension of chiefly residential districts.

Conservation, in relation to the environment, is, like pollution, an 'in' word these days. It means something more than preservation, which was an 'in' word of the 1920s and 1930s. Preservation implies static protection, saving from decay, keeping things as they are. Conservation means, or has come to mean, preserving purposefully : giving not merely continued existence but continued useful existence, which often implies retaining or restoring the traditional appearance of buildings, singly or in groups, but adapting the interior to modern uses. Conservation is also tending to be used in relation to areas and groups, whereas preservation is more often associated with individual buildings.

Conservation of the environment was not regarded as very important over the past century or so in Britain. Yet the practice, if not the word, was well known in earlier centuries of urban civilization, as has been noted in previous chapters. The Romans gave continued use in their towns to the urban fabric, and temples, theatres and other buildings, designed by Greek architects generations earlier. They also preserved obelisks, statues and other decorative features removed from ancient Egypt and elsewhere and transported over immense distances for re-erection in grandiose settings in Rome and other cities. Renaissance town-builders, a dozen centuries later, admired and maintained buildings surviving from classical Greece and Rome, and restored and modified them for continued use. Nineteenth-century town-builders destroyed much of the inherited environment to make way for their own buildings and other land uses. But, as if in repentance for so much destruction, they were often over-enthusiastic in restoring old buildings, especially those of medieval origin. Their zeal was such as to bring into being a society whose aim was to protect old buildings from the excesses both of those who wanted to destroy them and those who wanted to 'restore' them. William Morris, in the manifesto that led to the founding of the Society for the Protection of Ancient Buildings (1877), deplored attempts to 'bring a building back to its best time in history' by means of stripping away the various alterations and additions made to it in varying styles throughout the centuries of its existence:

> It is for all these buildings, therefore, of all times and styles, that we plead, and call upon those who have to deal with them to put Protection in the place of Restoration, to stave off decay by daily care, to prop a perilous wall or mend a leaky roof by such means as are obviously meant for support or covering, and show no pretence of other art, and otherwise to resist all tampering with either the fabric or ornament of the building as it stands; if it has become inconvenient for its present use, to raise another building rather than alter or enlarge the old one;* in fine, to treat our ancient buildings as monuments of a bygone art, created by bygone manners, that modern art cannot meddle with without destroying ... thus only can we protect our ancient buildings, and hand them down instructive and venerable to those that come after us.

Until recent years conservation was scarcely recognized as a subject for national government policy. Buildings and ground layouts from the past survived fortuitously, largely on their own merits, and chiefly because they could continue to serve useful purposes. Although much has been lost in the cause of logical and necessary redevelopment, urban environments can still show examples of all times and styles: the legacy from medieval builders includes churches, revered and cared for by generations of worshippers, guildhalls and town halls whose architectural merit, sound construction and usable accommodation justified retention, and the many houses, great and small, sometimes associated with great names and great events, sometimes with neither, which continue in use, occasionally unsuspected behind Georgian façades or beneath modern cladding. From Queen Anne and Georgian builders came the elegant and practical residential terraces, crescents and squares, and public buildings, whose efficiency, setting and sheer good design merited survival and, indeed, continue generally to be

* The Society's committee later added a note of clarification concerning this clause.

meticulously maintained and copied for use at the present time. From Victorian builders came those never-to-be-repeated essays of grandeur in conception and courage in construction, some of which deserve to remain as inspiration (if not for emulation) for architects of today and tomorrow. From Edwardian and inter-war builders, similarly, have come buildings of all kinds, without some of which our townscapes would be much the poorer; and, doubtless, before this century is out some of the achievements of recent times, such as Centre Point, the Royal Festival Hall and the Hayward Gallery, will be candidates for preservation on grounds of architectural interest or notoriety. Clearly, many buildings of past ages must give place to new ones designed to meet particular requirements of the present time; but, equally clearly, a case can be made for retaining good examples of past achievements to enrich the quality and variety of townscapes.

Architectural merit is not the only consideration in the case for conservation. Evidence of a sentimental interest in the past has accumulated in recent years. This is not false sentiment, but a genuinely increasing interest in the works and the ways of earlier generations. It is seen in renewed enthusiasm for collecting and using antique furniture and *objets d'art*, even Victorian trivia or Art Nouveau items which, a few years ago, languished unloved in lofts. Even more than furniture, *objets d'art* or books and documents, antique buildings as a visual expression of the life of a community excite the imagination and evoke the past for both residents and visitors. It may be true that the more mature a civilization becomes the more it delves into its past. It is certainly true that ancient civilizations rich in tangible evidence of history are of ever-increasing interest to modern tourists.

Britain's tremendous tourist industry thrives on visitors who are attracted not by climate or cuisine but by towns and buildings, panoply and pageantry, parks and countryside. Sentimental interest can arise from the direct association of buildings with events – for example the architecturally noble Tower of London and its ignoble history of violence and executions. It can also arise from the association of buildings with people, as with the architecturally undistinguished Chartwell and its most distinguished resident, Winston

Churchill, or a small house in Doughty Street, London, where Charles Dickens lived for some years.

Even fictitious associations can exert strong attraction: some visitors may still walk the length of London's Baker Street hoping to find number 221B; some still pay their respects to the Old Curiosity Shop (of doubtful authenticity) behind Kingsway. Sensitive action for conservation of the environment of streets and buildings is clearly of importance if such associations are to be maintained. The almost undisturbed continuity of modest little Doughty Street does much to maintain the authentic early-nineteenth-century atmosphere, although ill-mannered reconstruction of one house on the corner [53] is an affront to the street as a whole.

Prominent in the case for conservation of townscapes is the need to retain material evidence for scholarly investigation by urban historians and archaeologists. As Conzen noted, townscapes comprise three fundamental forms: the town plan or layout, the building

53. London: Doughty Street: a streetscape rudely interrupted by the corner house, rebuilt with no regard for the prevailing lines and shapes of windows.

fabric, and the pattern of land and building utilization, all of which are recordable and closely interrelated. Hence the whole townscape is of interest as a historical document: 'a kind of palimpsest on which the features contributed by any particular period may have been partly or wholly obliterated by those of a later one through the process of site succession or in some other way'.[1] Martin shared that view: 'Communities, like individuals, have their own subtleties, but so do the places that they inhabit. In some sort, a town is a document; it displays its history in its public face, as well as in its archives.'[2]

Conzen saw the town plan as comprising three elements: the streets and their mutual association in a street system; the individual land-parcels or plots and their aggregation in street blocks with distinct plot patterns; and the buildings, or more precisely their block plans, and the arrangement of these in the town plan as a whole. These complex elements in the townscape do not exist in isolation but are interconnected in the sense that each element conditions the others' origins, physical relations and functional significance, not just at present, but also in historical time. These elements are of fundamental interest to the urban historian and the archaeologist. Street patterns, plot shapes and boundaries, field boundaries, lines of former town walls and gates, market squares and their 'colonization' with encroaching structures, existing buildings and the foundations of their predecessors on the same sites – all these are the field data which experts need for advancing the understanding of urban history.

The refinement of methods and techniques of investigation used by such experts has advanced very significantly over the past half-century, and will surely do so even more rapidly in generations to come. If archaeologists of Victorian times, who through no fault of their own lacked the knowledge and experience of present-day professionals, had left more of their discoveries *in situ* and had destroyed less of what they deemed to be of no interest, modern researchers might have been able to extract more meaning from the past. Similarly, the finds that our generation may dismiss as unimportant could be of importance to our successors, who will probably be equipped to interpret them with greater understanding and confidence. Yet much urban archaeological evidence is being lost by redevelopment. Many historic towns are threatened by modern development, and the most important towns of all historical periods will be lost to archaeology in twenty years, if not before.[3]

It would obviously be advantageous for historical field studies if new development and redevelopment could take place within, or with maximum regard for, the inherited structure of plot boundaries, streets, lanes and courtyards. In some cases such a constraint may prove unreasonable or impracticable for new building or road developments; in others it might be achieved with a measure of sympathy on the part of developers and of ingenuity on that of their architects. In yet others a compromise might have to be reached, as in the case of the Temple of Mithras and Bucklersbury House, London.

The events of the past two decades have stimulated increasing support for conservation. Ruthless commercial operations, aided by weak or uncomprehending planning control and traffic 'improvements', have resulted in the destruction of many hundreds of fine buildings and the crude widening and opening-up of areas, in city and town centres especially, whose street and footpath patterns were admirably suited to people going about their daily business on foot. In 1964 the ancient cathedral city of Worcester, with a legacy of fine buildings of modest scale on a delicate medieval pattern of streets and places, underwent a major operation of shocking and needless severity. Almost before the patient knew what was happening or had time to protest, it was virtually subjected to heart and lung transplants, and now suffers chronic loss of memory. Gloucester, Lincoln and Abingdon are among other small towns whose historic central areas have been very roughly treated by redevelopment. Similar operations of varying degrees of severity have been inflicted, by public authorities as well as commercial developers, on the national capital, on provincial capitals, cathedral cities, county towns – anywhere that promised a profit. The list of good buildings and street layouts lost is lamentably long. Up till 1967 some 400 listed* buildings were being destroyed each year, together with unknown numbers of unlisted buildings which, though

* By the Ministry of Housing and Local Government : see later.

of no great individual merit, combined with others to give strength of character to their setting.

Three random examples suggest the scope of destruction : half of a fine medieval shop in St Albans, lopped off to ease a bend in a main road in the (futile) hope of speeding the progress of heavy traffic which should not be encouraged there anyway ; the graceful Georgian Woburn Square, which is being demolished in stages to make way for uncongenial teaching accommodation, thus increasing the very substantial losses already inflicted on that fine Bloomsbury estate by London University ; and London's unique Victorian Coal Exchange, most notable for its round tower and its domed interior court, described thus by Hitchcock : 'Inside this court ... no masonry at all was visible. One saw only an elegant cage of iron elements rising to the glazed hemisphere above. The metal members were richly but appropriately detailed, and there was even more appropriate decorative painting by Sang in such panels as were not glazed.'[4] The Coal Exchange was demolished in 1963 because it stood where traffic engineers wanted to widen a road which is still not completed.

As Hermione Hobhouse has so clearly shown,[5] London's losses have been savage and in many cases easily avoidable. In nearly every city and town, however, buildings standing on town-centre sites of potentially high commercial value disappeared one by one or block by block as a result of skilfully organized operations by developers who acknowledge no responsibility for existing architectural or historical merit. The buildings that replace them, whether multiples, chain-stores, supermarkets, office blocks or flats, are often remarkably undistinguishable one from another, no matter who 'designed' them or in which town they make their appearance. Utilitarian, flat-faced, monotonous, lightweight, they contribute very little of benefit to existing urban character and show scant respect for prevailing styles or local building materials. Their designers, often disregarding traditional vertical emphasis in façades that arose from an urban fabric of narrow-frontage plots, make their new buildings straddle two or more adjacent plots, thus introducing a pronounced and alien horizontal emphasis [54].

54. *Reading: Broad Street; unsympathetic horizontal accent in a street of mainly vertical accent.*

Nearly as distressing for townscapes as the demolition of good buildings is their survival in a mutilated state. Mutilation often stems from a change in the use for which the building was originally designed. Change from house to shop has often been beneficial in giving continued useful life to a building and a profitable return on site value. But where structural alterations have been made with little heed to the qualities of the building, changes of use have resulted in damage and deterioration in townscapes.

A second glance at some buildings in established shopping streets reveals their origin as Georgian detached houses or terraces [55]. Their former front gardens, if deep enough, provided space for single-storey shop protrusions and possibly a widened pavement; or, if the garden depth was insufficient, large plate-glass windows replaced the former delicately glazed front windows of the house. Some Victorian owners, making modifications to several adjacent houses at a time, succeeded in producing pleasant and useful shop

55. *London: Holland Park Avenue, Georgian terraced houses adapted for shops and petrol filling station.*

premises with a nice sense of order and continuity. But conversions made in piecemeal fashion to one or two properties at different times brought a confusion of shapes and sizes of shop interspersed with houses still recognizable in their original form, but with shabby and neglected approaches and façades. Change from house to shop is not always a one-way process, however: when shops lose custom owing to a shift in the trading location they are often beneficially converted to residential use.

Change from residential to office use has occurred very frequently in recent times. The change can involve an extensive district, like London's Mayfair, or a few properties at a time along streets that have gained commercial importance. Conversion from house to office is usually less visually unfortunate than from house to shop. Town houses of architectural or historical interest can make very satisfactory offices, whether 'prestige' headquarters of important business concerns, such as stately seventeenth-century Schomberg

Townscapes

House in London's Pall Mall, or small houses along High Streets that do good service for firms of professionals such as solicitors, architects, surveyors, accountants and dentists. Many fine and rather large town houses that proved uneconomic for residential use have been acquired by local authorities for their departments – borough treasurer, engineer, health clinic – and used with the minimum of alteration. Such buildings can deteriorate if too many people are crammed into them: for example, the fine former drawing-room or dining-room that would serve admirably as the office of the senior partner of a firm of solicitors, would probably lose its elegance in accommodating a typing pool or a team of health inspectors complete with steel filing cabinets and office cupboards. Planning control rarely succeeds in preventing such deterioration.

Town houses along shopping streets can also respond well to use as restaurants, coffee shops, clubs or hotels, but conversion to less suit-

56. *Truro: Assembly Rooms (1772), used as garages, workshop and gown shop, townscape completed with twin telephone boxes, traffic signs and municipal gardening, all at the doors of the Cathedral.*

able purposes, such as garages and petrol filling stations [55, 56], can produce appalling results. Other changes to a very different use can succeed in conserving a good architectural façade as an adornment to the townscape: for example, that of a redundant church or chapel. Churches have been successfully converted for use as exhibition centres; chapels can make satisfactory auction rooms, and one was adapted as a swimming pool with the vestry as men's changing-rooms, the choir stalls as ladies' changing-rooms and the gallery as refreshment room. Sudbury's Corn Exchange has been converted to a branch library; Saffron Walden's is following suit; Basingstoke's is now a flourishing theatre. An eighteenth-century mill and oasthouses in London's East End [57] now provide open-plan offices, board-rooms and other accommodation for a staff of 260 persons. Winchester's Wharf Mill (with the addition of a wing in sympathetic design) has become fifteen flats. Leed's Coal Exchange is being

57. *London: Bromley-by-Bow: Clock Mill and oasthouses, now accommodating the clerical staff of a brewery. This conversion is likely to encourage rehabilitation of other buildings in the vicinity.*

transformed into a concert hall; would that London's could have been given some congenial use.

Wherever an old building permits a measure of flexibility in the use of its space, possibilities present themselves for conversion to some useful purpose. It is comparatively rarely that inflexibility defeats ingenuity, but it could do so in, for example, a Gothic church, some music halls, railway stations, and similar structures designed for a specialist purpose. The Government publication *New Life for Old Buildings*[6] illustrates twenty-two examples of restoration and conversion.

Action towards defining, developing and implementing the case for conservation can come (as Sir Hugh Casson put it) '... from all of us. Central Government for advice, finance and legislation; Local Government for policy and executive action; and the rest of us acting as a creative nuisance.'[7] Central government's lead was until recent years, although neither exemplary nor determined, probably a fair reflection of an apathetic public opinion. Its lead in legislation was also slow in starting and only became really useful by the late 1960s, when much irreversible damage had been done.

Following the efforts of William Morris and others, the principle of protecting and preserving buildings was established in the form of the Ancient Monuments Protection Act, 1882, which empowered the Commissioners of Works to accept as a gift or bequest, to purchase, or to accept guardianship of ancient monuments, which for the most part were regarded as 'ancient structures except those that are inhabited otherwise than by a caretaker or are buildings in use for ecclesiastical purposes'. In practice, this meant keeping prehistoric camps, stone circles and barrows, and the remains of abbeys, castles and bridges, as well as some relatively modern structures like the iron bridge at Ironbridge, Shropshire. Inhabited houses were not included until provision was made in the Town and Country Planning Act of 1932 to prevent demolition, but not mutilation; and until recent times the principal legislation for protecting buildings was that afforded by the 1944 and 1947 Acts.

Under this legislation the Minister was, and still is, required to compile lists of buildings of special architectural or historic interest. A provisional list was first prepared, in which buildings were divided into categories. Grade I consisted of buildings of outstanding interest; Grade II comprised buildings of special interest which warranted every effort being made to preserve them, the most important among them being classified Grade II*; Grade III was for buildings which did not qualify for the statutory list by the standards current when the list was compiled, but which were important enough to be drawn to the attention of local authorities and others so that the case for preserving them could be considered.

The criteria for listing were discussed in detail in 'Instructions to Investigators for Listing Buildings of Special Architectural or Historic Interest' (under Section 42 of the Town and Country Planning Act, 1944). For this purpose, inspectors were advised to consider a building –

(1) which may be regarded as a work of art, 'the product of a distinct and outstanding creative mind';

(2) which, although not a distinct creation in this sense, possesses the characteristic virtues of the school of design that produced it;

(3) which qualifies on aesthetic grounds as an 'outstanding composition of fragmentary beauties welded together by time and good fortune';

(4) which forms a link in the chain of architectural development;

(5) which is a link in the history of structural technique: a product of the mechanical and industrial revolution such as an iron bridge, a cast-iron-and-glass conservatory, etc.;

(6) which is of earlier date than 1725 and largely intact; of date 1725–1800, 'though selection will be necessary'; 1800–1850, confined to buildings 'of definite quality and character'; 1850–1914, 'only outstanding works'; and, since 1914, 'none, unless the case seems very strong';

(7) which is of interest to historians, archaeologists and tourists;

(8) which forms part of a group of architectural or historic interest.

The authors of this document acknowledge that 'an attempt like this to express in words what cannot be so expressed must necessarily dwell disproportionately on abnormal and borderline cases ... but that the great bulk ... will probably deal with clear examples of fine buildings and...numerically the 18th century will...have a clear preponderance over any other'. New criteria are adopted as standards of taste change; for example buildings of post-1914 date which are of great distinction, which act as focal points, or which have interiors of special interest, are now included.

These lists, compilation of which represents a great achievement by a small team of inspectors, contain brief descriptions of the buildings and are known as 'provisional lists'. After administrative discussion (but not discussion on merit) with the local authorities concerned, buildings graded I, II and III were placed on statutory lists which contain neither grading nor description. Buildings graded III were included in supplementary lists which accompanied the statutory lists. Anyone seeking to demolish a building on the statutory list or to alter or extend it in a way that would seriously affect its character was required to give two months written notice to the local planning authority, who in turn had to notify the Minister; it was then open to the local planning authority or the district council to make a 'building preservation order'.

The effect of such an order, which had to be confirmed by the Minister, was to prohibit the demolition or serious alteration of the building without the express permission of the authority who made the order. Any building of special interest, on the statutory list or not, could be made the subject of a building preservation order; and the local authority could acquire compulsorily a building for which a building preservation order was in force if it was not being properly maintained.

This procedure saved many fine buildings that would otherwise have been destroyed, but was effective only in respect of individual buildings [58] – not groups or areas as a whole. Moreover, if neither the local planning authority nor the Minister acted within the short period of two months the building could be destroyed or irretrievably altered. Because the emphasis on preserving the individual building, rather than groups of buildings and their settings, areas like Bloomsbury[8] were gradually eroded, and some historic towns were redeveloped in a way that very much degraded their historic character and their appearance. Public opinion, too, had not yet learned to value its architectural and historic heritage, and was unconcerned to see

58. *London: Great West Road: Hogarth's House (eighteenth century), brutally hemmed in by factories and an urban motorway.*

historic buildings disappear at the rate of about 400 a year – rather more than one every day.

In 1964 the Council for British Archaeology entered the conservation arena with a declaration of welcome to the Buchanan Report, especially to its statement that, in historic cities, retaining 'a major part of the heritage of the English-speaking world' will impose even greater restraint and inconvenience on the motorist. The Council observed that the prospect of enormously increased expenditure on urban roads called for special attention to the preservation of historic street-plans as well as buildings of special interest. In its view the creation of environmental areas, as recommended in *Traffic in Towns*, could often be facilitated by retaining an ancient pattern of streets; thus areas in historic towns which ought to be preserved on account of their buildings and/or their street patterns should be listed and graded in the same manner as individual buildings under current legislation. The Government grant system should accordingly be so designed as to give local authorities the maximum assistance in dealing with traffic problems in small towns as well as large.

In the following year the CBA published its *List of Historic Towns*. There were 324 of these, selected from an initial list of 660, each of which possessed not only buildings of historic or architectural importance but also historic street-plans. Even though a medieval street pattern may retain hardly any buildings of medieval origin, its medieval quality – expressed in street-widths, informal spaces and the scale of its buildings – persists and forms an essential ingredient in the quality of the town [12, 14]. The inclusion of any town in this list is, to quote the CBA's memorandum, 'an argument for preparing for it a comprehensive survey of the *historic environment, illustrating its layout, its historic buildings, its urban quality and any other special characteristics. This "heritage plan" should, with the "transportation plan" suggested in the Buchanan Report, form an obligatory part of the development plan process and should make specific provision for the conservation of the features emphasized by the survey.'*

Possibly bearing in mind the devastation so recently wrought on the centre of Worcester, the CBA singled out 51 of the towns on its list as being so splendid and so precious that proposals affecting their historic centres should be decided directly by the Minister rather than by their local authorities. The CBA acknowledged that making a list was a risky step which implied that towns omitted were not worth a second thought; but they accepted the risk in order not to make the list so long as to be impractical. The Government backed the particular proposal about the 51 special towns only to the extent of contributing towards the cost of pilot surveys for four of the finest on the list – Bath, Chester, Chichester and York.[9]

Much of the CBA's advice regarding the protection of areas, as well as individual buildings, of historic or architectural interest was given effect shortly afterwards, however, with the passing of the Civic Amenities Act in 1967. This Act required local planning authorities 'to determine which parts of their areas are of special architectural or historic interest, the character or appearance of which it is desirable to preserve or enhance'. Such areas might then be designated as 'Conservation Areas', and the planning authority would have to pay 'special attention' to applications for development within them. New buildings, alterations and additions to existing buildings (especially listed ones), changes of use, advertisements, street furniture and street patterns would all be subject to 'special scrutiny'.

The intention is not that conservation areas should be preserved unaltered, embalmed, or made into museum pieces; they should be enabled to continue as useful and functional elements of the town, retaining their traditional character and appearance [59]. New development will be necessary from time to time to keep them alive and useful, but new buildings must respect existing forms, materials, colours, roof-lines, skylines, and the environment generally.

Despite the encouraging spirit of this legislation, local planning authorities gained no new powers: they were merely required to consider whether proposals for development would 'preserve or enhance the character and appearance' of a conservation area. Several loopholes remained. Authorities continued to receive applications to demolish listed buildings. Some came from owners who wished to

59. *Leeds: 'pedestrianized' streets in a Conservation Area, with most buildings retained but some replaced where necessary; variety in floorscape.*

redevelop a site and could see no useful purpose in retaining their existing buildings, but many were from owners who could neither afford to undertake the necessary repairs nor find a purchaser able or willing to do so. Since failure to comply with a provisional Building Preservation Order meant liability to a fine not exceeding £100, whereas loss of opportunity to demolish and redevelop could mean forgoing very substantial gain, such Orders were often defied. 'Accidents', too, could occur: a crane or heavy lorry could brush against the corner of a listed building and cause damage (described as 'coup de bulldozer') which could not be remedied at reasonable cost; roof tiles could be dislodged or windows broken to admit the elements and speed the process of decay.

Owners who had given notice of intention to demolish listed buildings and had received no decision from the local planning authority within two months were free to proceed, and usually lost no time in doing so. Where a local authority refused consent to demolish or make substantial alterations, applicants could appeal to the Minister and launch long-drawn-out legal wrangles which they could afford, in view of their potential profit, but which understaffed authorities were often anxious to avoid.

Another discouragement to conservation lay in the provision that, if a Building Preservation Order were made enforceable, an owner could claim to be thereby deprived of beneficial use of his land and could compel the authority to purchase the building and pay the market price for the site. Such a site might have very high potential value for shop or office development and attract high compensation. Here, too, was a field for long legal wrangling; and even if the authority won the day it would end up with possession of a good, though not very profitable, building, much expenditure of professional skills and a heavy bill for compensation.

The Town and Country Planning Act, 1968, abolished the cumbersome Building Preservation Order, with its inadequate two-month period of notice to demolish, and substituted the 'Listed Building Consent' which requires an owner to obtain specific written consent before any demolition or alteration may take place. Unlisted buildings previously subject to Building Preservation Orders are now deemed to be listed. If a local authority is the owner, it cannot grant itself permission to demolish, but must obtain the Minister's consent. This Act introduced more effective discouragement to the flaunting of laws by enabling courts to impose fines for unauthorized demolition having regard to the financial benefit likely to accrue to the developer in consequence of the offence. As an alternative or addition, prison sentences of up to twelve months can be imposed.

The Act also stipulated that before allowing demolitions or alterations local authorities must consult certain bodies, including the Ancient Monuments Society, the Council for British Archaeology, the Society for the Protection of Ancient Buildings, the Georgian Group, the Victorian Society, the Royal Commission on Historical Monuments and certain civic societies. Administrative action was taken shortly after the Act came into force to eliminate the Supplementary or Grade III list, which had always been regarded as praise with faint damnation. In revising the lists, Ministry Inspectors would upgrade most of the good Grade IIIs to II, and would notify the remainder to local authorities as being of local interest and merit.

The Town and Country Planning Act, 1971, consolidated and re-enacted most of the current planning legislation including the 1968 Act described above and the Civic Amenities Act; but loopholes still remained. Unlisted buildings in conservation areas were still without protection, even though their quality, as single buildings, groups or even whole streets, could contribute much to the character and quality of the area. The T & CP (Amendment) Act 1971, enabled local planning authorities to prevent the demolition (though not alteration, such as removal of a shop-front) of buildings or groups of special architectural importance whose preservation is essential to the character of a conservation area.

The Town and Country Amenities Act of 1974 advanced the cause of conservation still further. It provides that no unlisted building (other than a shed or other minor structure) in a conservation area may be demolished without consent granted by the local authority or, in cases where the local authority wishes to demolish, without consent from the Secretary of State for the Environment. The Act imposes upon local authorities the duty to draw up and publish proposals for the preservation and enhancement of conservation areas, and to submit such proposals to a public meeting. It also gives

Townscapes

power to the Secretary of State to make separate regulations for the control of advertisements in conservation areas.

This Act makes important new provision for the basis of compensation when listed buildings are acquired compulsorily by a local authority for preservation. Payment will be for the value of the listed building only, and not for the value of the site for redevelopment. Local authorities may thus serve repair notices without the possible consequence of having to purchase the building. They may also recover costs incurred in carrying out urgent works to unoccupied listed buildings; and this power may also be extended to unlisted buildings in conservation areas if the Secretary of State so directs.

Pursuing Hugh Casson's allocation of roles in conservation ('Central Government for advice, finance and legislation; Local Government for policy and executive action; and the rest of us acting as a creative nuisance'), central government has improved its performance in recent years. It has offered good advice in publications.[10] It has made increasingly generous finance available both for the Historic Buildings Councils and local authorities. And, as already noted, it has produced effective legislation.

The performance of local authorities in terms of policy and executive action has been uneven and disappointing. They have shown enthusiasm for conservation in principle by declaring their policy, designating more than 3,000 Conservation Areas and publishing plans purporting to show how 'preservation and enhancement' of such areas is to be secured. Executive action to implement the policy in terms of more than a few buildings at a time, however, easily escapes observation.

A few towns with important roles in the tourist industry have acted energetically. The Greater London Council and its predecessor, the London County Council, clapped on many preservation orders and imposed stronger controls on development. Windsor has given its High Street the third 'face-lift' since 1961 and keeps much of the central core (declared a Conservation Area) as bright as a new pin. York has cleaned and restored many buildings and 'pedestrianized' some streets, and is pressing ahead with the important Aldwark Conservation Area. Winchester has removed wheeled traffic from a large part of its High Street for the first time in ten centuries, and

Lincoln has done likewise. Cities and towns with active councils, prodding civic societies and interested ratepayers have promoted town schemes, gaining a share of the cost of restoring groups of historic buildings from the Historic Buildings Councils. Leeds, divesting itself of centuries of soot and discovering a fine legacy of Victorian buildings, offices, warehouses and mills, is beginning to see itself as a place of historic architectural interest capable of attracting tourists. Much of Bewdley's central area has been affectionately restored and Lax Street, a complete street of artisan houses dating from Georgian times, is being treated not as a slum for demolition but as an asset for conversion and continued use.

But in many cases, above all of cities and towns that are not manifestly beautiful but nevertheless still pleasant to look at and live in and work in, local councils seem to show little interest in action for conservation. Despite their designations of Conservation Areas, they continually acquiesce in the destruction of buildings of character and quality and give consent for replacement by big, brutish blocks alien to the tradition and identity of the place. They agree to street widenings and traffic 'improvement' schemes which fail to improve but succeed in obliterating more of the urban fabric. They tolerate proliferating traffic signs and clutter of street furniture.

The inference seems to be that many councils, and often the planning officers who advise them, look upon conservation as something intended only for towns of distinction, such as those listed by the Council for British Archaeology, but not for the ordinary workaday environment.* It may be that the only way to halt this continued undervaluing and loss of individuality and tradition is for the central government to take the CBA's advice to remove responsibility for conservation from local authorities and take mandatory powers of implementation.

As for Hugh Casson's role for 'the rest of us', it is difficult to gauge the strength of public support for conservation. At the local level it can suddenly emerge if a situation demands it, and recede as rapidly

---

*Individual planning officers have expressed a typical view: 'Ours is a "working town" and we think that money and effort is better devoted to such unspoilt places as — rather than here.' (This despite the fact that the 'working town' in question has much in the way of good architectural heritage and layout.)

if the situation is resolved. Although most people show interest in the appearance of their own homes and gardens, they show less interest in their residential environment and less still in the places where they work or do their shopping. Their reaction to authorities or private developers who cause changes, beneficial or otherwise, in the environment is largely indifference, or resignation to the inevitable. Of those people who do notice adverse changes, few seem prepared to do more than grumble, and fewer still to take action. Nevertheless the few who do care about adverse changes have taken an increasingly effective part in trying to modify or minimize their effects. Environmental problems, being essentially local in character, call for solutions to be worked out at local level rather than imposed by a remote authority. Demolition of familiar buildings and their replacement with dull or brash or brutish blocks, building-over of private open spaces hitherto enjoyed (if only visually) by the public, re-routing of heavy traffic flows, giving market places and other public spaces over to car-parking—these are examples of changes that can arouse waves of resentment in a local environment, though scarcely a ripple in the wider environment of a district, county or region.

Local action is prompted by the efforts of local people acting in concert as a civic society, amenity society, history society, residents' association or other group. Such people share a common interest in keeping their environment in the condition in which they as residents, possibly of long standing, think it should be kept. They are usually middle class, more elderly than youthful, more indignant than aggressive, inured to public apathy and official reproach. Their patience and persistence over the years has been rewarded with much disappointment, some quiet achievement and the occasional real triumph in saving parts of the townscape from spoliation, finding new and useful life for threatened buildings of architectural or historic interest, whether cottage or stately home, shop or town hall, and generally defending the pleasantness and habitability of their environment.

Small local societies often encountered problems that they could neither solve from their own resources nor make known to a sufficiently wide or influential public. In 1957 the then Minister for Housing and Local Government, Duncan Sandys, seeing the need to coordinate and strengthen the work of such groups, established the

Conservation of the urban environment

Civic Trust as an independent and unofficial body backed with government funds only during its formative years. The Trust's aims were, and still are, to encourage high quality in architecture and planning; to preserve buildings of distinction and protect rural beauty; and to inspire civic pride and public interest in the environment. It supports the work of local societies with professional advice and 'know-how' and gives executive assistance where requested. It operates an awards scheme for outstanding examples of design in buildings and layouts, organizes conferences on environmental matters, and publishes views and reports on urgent questions. Of many initiatives and achievements in a short and active existence, two in particular merit mention.

The first, the 1958 'face-lift' of Magdalen Street, Norwich, led some eighty shopkeepers and other property owners to act in concert to improve a street which contained buildings of character but which had become 'submerged in a jumble of discordant shopfronts, a clutter of advertisements and traffic signs, and a network of overhead wires ... and a despressing drabness due to the neglect of colour'.[11] Having consulted the City Engineer, local architects, the bus company and others concerned, the Trust launched the scheme, in the course of which the following was accomplished:

66 properties were repainted; 38 nameboards relettered or otherwise improved, 22 projecting signs removed, 26 awnings replaced by others of gayer colours, cornice lighting installed on one important building and the church floodlit, two bus shelters of improved design erected, a number of traffic notices combined or dispensed with altogether, so reducing their number from 30 to 13, a variety of misplaced advertisements and other unsightly objects removed, overhead wires re-routed, and a waste plot planted as a garden. Excluding overdue repairs, the cost to shopkeepers and owners was around £5,000, an average of about £80 each.[11]

This idea of concerted action to improve street elevations caught on rapidly, not only in other Norwich streets but far and wide over the country. Burslem, Windsor and Edinburgh were among the first to prepare and implement 'face-lift' schemes within a year of the Norwich achievement; and within a decade about a hundred cities and towns had followed suit.

Another early and very important initiative taken by the Civic

139

Trust was to lead the Piccadilly Circus Inquiry. In 1959 a plan for redevelopment of a large part of the Circus, prepared by a property developer, approved in principle by the London County Council and other authorities and given publicity on television and in the press, aroused a furore of criticism. Architects, architectural students, letter-writers to *The Times* and a wide cross-section of opinion inveighed against the proposal; but as individuals they had neither the organization nor the resources to present an agreed case. The Trust took this opportunity, and marshalled the arguments along the lines that the proposed design was unworthy of such a famous site and that the Circus ought to be redeveloped as a whole and not piecemeal. After a hearing which became a *cause célèbre*, the Minister endorsed the arguments and rejected the plan.*

The Civic Trust was also instrumental in bringing the Civic Amenities Act to the Statute book in 1967; and it continues to be a powerful advocate both for conservation and for raising standards in new development. But with limited resources it can meet only the most urgent requests for aid. Local societies must continue to be vigilant and vociferous in defending townscapes against damage from developers and local councils alike. It says much for their spirit and determination that, despite apathy from the public and having only the slender resources of a very small membership, local societies continue to exercise a restraining influence over potential excesses in development. They have won the right to receive notification of development proposals from the local authorities, and, if their views do not always prevail, they do occasionally succeed in securing better results than might have ensued without their intervention and counsel.

* At the time of writing, fifteen years later, none of its many successors has been approved.

6: Rehabilitation, redevelopment and new development

Three kinds of 'treatment' for the restoration of good urban health were suggested at the beginning of the previous chapter. The second of these, central-area renewal, described as surgery to remove diseased parts and improve circulation in the urban body, has always been necessary for economically vigorous towns and cities, and is no less necessary at the present time.

The market response to demand for additional space for shops, offices and other town-centre accommodation is usually new buildings of greatly increased capacity concentrated in central locations. The response to demand for improved vehicle circulation and parking is usually street-widenings coupled with clearance of considerable areas of land for surface or multi-storey parking. Both these responses can obliterate wide areas of the inherited urban fabric, in some cases with little real disadvantage, but in others with regrettable architectural or historic loss. The greater a town's prosperity, the more acute the need for surgery; but the trouble is that healthy tissue is often removed, and enlarged arteries soon become clotted with the additional traffic they attract but fail to distribute satisfactorily to its various destinations.

The final responsibility for applying or permitting this treatment lies with the planning authority, who should seek, *inter alia*, to obtain the best possible reconciliation of the conflicting aims of accessibility and environmental quality as defined in the Buchanan Report. (As already noted, the 'Buchanan' cure can have unpleasant side-effects.) Achieving accessibility of various parts of the urban body to wheeled traffic means evolving a network of distributor and local roads. Achieving satisfactory environmental quality means arranging the spaces bounded by the distributor network (i.e. the 'environmental areas') to afford easy circulation for people on foot or in vehicles, and to obtain or retain safe, clean and pleasant conditions for everyday life.

The ideal environmental area is not penetrated by 'through' traffic, but only by traffic directly concerned with buildings within it. It has a predominant function, perhaps commercial or residential, or a series of compatible functions such as civic, cultural, educational, ecclesiastical, which can also accommodate other uses including those of shops, offices and housing. Thus, an ecclesiastical environmental area would be dominated by a cathedral and associated buildings such as houses for the clergy and administrators and a choir school; but it could also include restaurants, gift shops, antique shops and other facilities for visitors and tourists. A university environmental area would comprise faculty buildings, administrative block, library, assembly halls, churches, students' union and halls of residence, but also bookshops and other shops, branch banks and a pub or two. A commercial environmental area would ideally consist of shops, and possibly offices and restaurants, in the form of a 'pedestrian precinct' serviced from the rear, readily accessible from bus stops and railway station, and surrounded by car parks.

A precinct may be formed by closing a shopping street or group of streets to wheeled traffic and providing for servicing from the rear. This has been common practice on the European mainland for many years (especially good examples are to be found in German and Dutch cities), and is increasing in this country. Norwich's London Street is a highly successful (if over-publicized) case; Leeds has equally successful and more extensive areas in Bond Street and Commercial Street [59], and so have other British cities.

Quality of environment depends upon the degree to which disruptive effects of traffic – noise, fumes, dirt, danger and visual chaos – can be lessened or removed. But solving the traffic problem is only one factor. Important, too, are the presence or absence of nonconforming industrial uses; the design and finish of new buildings and their associated spaces; preservation of buildings of architectural or historic interest which confer character and continuity; the creation of places of calm and repose as well as vivacity and movement;

attention to detail in townscape and footscape; maintenance and renewal of trees, lawns and other planting.

Central-area redevelopment is subject to planning controls which should include application of plot ratios and daylighting codes. It also presents complex technical problems of design, construction and servicing of modern buildings. Architects have to contend with demands for buildings of greater height and floorspace, which use new methods of construction, building materials and servicing techniques, which may have to provide for special uses and accommodate complicated equipment, and which must still be reconciled with existing townscape, human needs and human scale.

The first major operation of modern comprehensive central-area redevelopment (started in the early 1950s) was the new shopping centre in the heart of war-damaged Coventry. The site, sloping east to west downhill from the city's main square, Broadgate, permitted an arrangement of shops on two levels in stepped terraces that formed a succession of squares flanking a broad pedestrian way. Footbridges linked shops on the upper level across the central axis, and squares were defined by low walls and flower beds. At the southern extremity is a circular market building with car-parking space on the roof. The layout functions admirably in accordance with the principles of the Buchanan Report, which it anticipated by some fifteen years. The shopping precinct is an environmental area, defined by distributor roads which enable buses, cars and service vehicles to arrive at, but not to penetrate, the precinct; shopping frontages are accessible only to pedestrians. Thus, for the first time, shoppers in the commercial heart of this city may pause from their shopping to sit and chat in the open air and look at pools, fountains, trees and pleasant floorscape, unharried by the danger, dirt and noise of motor vehicles. This distinguished composition in town planning was achieved with buildings which lack architectural distinction, which do not demand attention, but which enrich this ancient city with efficient, unpretentious modern townscape.

Coventry's precinct was the forerunner of many other operations in central-area redevelopment. War damage in such cities as Exeter, Plymouth and Southampton was so extensive as to make retention of much of the previous fabric of streets, lanes and spaces impracticable. But whereas Coventry's planners took the opportunity to segregate routes of travel for vehicles and pedestrians, the central areas of Exeter, Plymouth and Southampton emerged from the ruins in architectural dress of new materials but essentially pre-war cut.

Birmingham's tremendous achievement in central-area redevelopment showed scant regard for the existing fabric, much of which was obliterated along with several buildings of architectural merit. But the solution for traffic was triumphant. The inner ring-road has relieved the central core of much extraneous traffic without constituting an impenetrable barrier to pedestrians, who can reach the core via numerous underpasses. An interesting new townscape feature was the use of space underneath roundabouts for groups of shops. The most arresting achievement is the vast shopping and office complex, the biggest of its kind in the country, which arose on the site of the old market, the Bull Ring. As in Coventry, the layout functions with streamlined ease. The various parts – the open market, shops on two levels, offices in towers and slabs, bus terminal and multi-storey car park – are readily approached by buses, cars and service vans with no interference to the progress of people on foot. The shops and market are also readily accessible from long-established shopping streets in the vicinity, as a result of well-planned continuity between old and new frontages. Again, the architecture is far from distinguished; it comprises mostly monotonous shopping façades and crude cubes of office development, but has a vigorous visual relief in the Rotunda, a twenty-four-storey cylindrical tower of offices.

A major central-area scheme for the historic area immediately to the north of London's St Paul's Cathedral produced a townscape of typically mid-twentieth-century flavour. The essence of any plan for such a sensitive area would be to make good use of the extremely valuable land adjoining the City's commercial heart, whilst ensuring the continued visual dominance of the City's grandest architectural possession – which had miraculously escaped war damage. The plan adopted succeeded in not leaving the cathedral in draughty, stately isolation, and in effecting a smooth integration of its immediate surroundings with the ancient commercial heart via a pedestrian

Rehabilitation, redevelopment and new development

precinct of comparatively narrow lanes and smallish squares [60]. The development comprises shops, and some restaurants, at ground level, with offices above and also in independent blocks. The planning restrictions on height and bulk of new buildings were designed to allow adequate provision of floor-space without causing any diminution in the visual dominance of the cathedral. The perceptive relationship between heights of buildings and dimensions of passages and open places affords some compensation for the coldness and severity of most of the elevations.

The redevelopments at Coventry and Birmingham represent an impressive response to changes in the retailing process. The modern, large-scale urban shopping centre, an amalgam of street market, high street and department store, provides for shoppers in thousands. It fills car-boots as well as shopping baskets; it is replenished by mobile warehouses of vast size. It has qualified as an accepted element in modern townscape, and its visual impact is of great significance. Sheer size and bulk make it impressive, whether expressed as

60. *London: St Paul's precinct, 1961–7. Interconnecting squares with shops and restaurants on ground level and offices above or in separate blocks. Frontages accessible to pedestrians only; garaging and service access for vehicles at the rear of, or below, business premises.*

commonplace cuboids of concrete, aluminium, glass and plastic, or as brutal cliffs and caverns of concrete like Portsmouth's dismal Tricorn Centre, or as a massive and magnificent bastion of commerce like Montreal's Place Bonaventure.

Smaller versions of town-centre shopping and office complexes all over the country are less impressive, but not only because of their smaller size. The most usual form for such a centre is essentially a straight footway, or 'mall', some 25 feet wide, flanked by shops of standard frontage, with 'magnet' stores at either end to ensure, if possible, that shoppers pass all frontages. The layout is compact, in order to keep walking distances to the minimum; and even greater compactness is achieved by two-level shops. The office element, where present, can be premises above shops, or a slab or cube. The centres vary in attractiveness. Some, such as the early example at Blackburn, the maturing one at Romford and the recent Butts Centre at Reading, are important features in the townscape. Some are comparatively undemonstrative because they have been skilfully integrated into the existing urban fabric, as at Dorchester or Chester. Some are intruders in indifferent modern dress which have wiped out wide swathes of historic townscape, as at Worcester and Gloucester. Old towns need the benefit of new commercial developments; but old townscapes will gain maximum benefit if large new developments can be concentrated in planned locations – on sites cleared of unsatisfactory and uneconomic buildings, or on back land – which will enable existing groups of buildings of merit to continue to serve useful purposes.

Another powerful element in modern central-area redevelopment, especially in the capital and large provincial cities, is the large hotel. 'De luxe' hotels of Edwardian and Victorian days – Ritz, Savoy, Piccadilly, Waldorf, Russell – enriched the urban scene with their elegant and affluent air [39]. With few exceptions, the large modern hotel makes singularly unattractive townscape. Recent rapid development of the tourist industry, including what Tony Aldous calls 'Package Tour Pollution',[1] in London especially, has stimulated a tremendous demand for bedspaces and led to hasty development with insufficient consideration of, inter alia, the effect of tall and bulky buildings on the scene.

Rehabilitation, redevelopment and new development

Architects of earlier days seemed to observe the principle that, as a large building is likely to be seen from many standpoints in the town, it should be designed and built to be worth seeing. This principle has evidently been ignored in recent decades. So many office blocks are no more visually stimulating than the filing cabinets they hold [6]; and, equally, many hotels are seen to comprise cubicles by the hundred within a vast cuboid container – for example, the flat, vacuous Post House Hotel at the entrance to London Airport from the M4.

Two problems to be solved are, first, the tendency to increasing giantism in hotel administration; and second, how to reduce the impact of sheer bulk and height in townscape and skyscape. A recent success in the last respect was scored by the designers of the Tower Hotel, next to Tower Bridge, London, in the adoption of a cruciform ground plan with arms stepped up to a central point, giving the impression of a group or cluster of separate, though similar, buildings.

The third of the 'treatments' referred to at the beginning of this chapter was that involving rehabilitation, redevelopment and extension of chiefly residential districts. Attitudes towards rehabilitation and redevelopment in the housing field have changed drastically over the past decade. The popular prescription for new development in the 1950s and 1960s was wholesale clearance of slums and outdated housing in inner-city areas, and new building in the form of flats in tower blocks and slabs, interspersed sometimes with four-storey maisonettes and three- and two-storey houses. Towers and slabs often produced not only an overbearing, inhuman townscape, but unhappy and sometimes disastrous social conditions for the families filed away, as it were, in vast filing-cabinet-shaped buildings.*

The precedent set by the Deeplish Study[3] encouraged a shift of emphasis in Britain from rebuilding to rehabilitation. Amended housing legislation provided incentives for reconditioning properties that merited it, rather than sweeping them away for replacement by new buildings. The 1969 Housing Act introduced the 'General

*An extreme example was the massive Pruitt–Igoe development of 2,762 apartments in 33 eleven-storey slabs for about 10,000 people in St Louis, USA, such a disastrous failure that it was demolished after only twenty years of occupation.[2]

Improvement Area' (GIA) procedure and authorized grants for reconditioning individual dwellings of up to £1,000 per dwelling, payable by local authorities to owners. It also provided for a contribution from the Secretary of State for the Environment towards the cost of making these grants, which are not restricted to GIAs, but are available to landowners generally, and also towards the cost of improving the environment in those areas.* Social surveys made in several large cities during the late 1960s indicated a clear preference among residents in old inner districts for remaining in them rather than moving to new flats or houses on the outskirts.

The Barker End estate, built in Bradford during the 1880s and one of many recent GIAs, comprised a typical grid of streets of 'bye-law' type lined with long terraces of two-storey houses solidly constructed in local stone with slate roofs. Each house had a small backyard with access to the 'sanitary lane'. Sand-blasting and re-pointing the stone, replacing defective parts and re-painting and modernizing interiors brought a new appearance and vitality to the dwellings. Of great significance, too, were the environmental improvements. For the first time, residents can see trees and grass from their windows, and can sit outside on summer days in strips of open space that flow over what were street intersections. These improvements were made by a rearrangement of the pattern of streets, retaining those necessary for traffic circulation and parking-space, and closing the inessential ones for conversion to open space. The proposed rearrangement was set out initially with chalk, string and railway sleepers, so that residents could try it out and make their own suggestions before the permanent change was made. Residents showed obvious pride and delight in their modernized homes and the greatly improved surroundings.

Swindon's Railway Village, made up of some 300 terraced houses built in the 1840s for employees of the Great Western Railway, was

*The amount of contribution was to equal 75%, or in some special cases 90%, of the annual loan charges for 20 years in respect of the grants made by local authorities for reconditioning ('standard', 'special' and 'improvement' grants); and 50% in respect of expenditure, not exceeding £100 per dwelling (raised to £200 in 1972) by local authorities themselves on improving the environment in a GIA. (See also *West's Law of Housing*, Third Edition, 1974.)

in rather a decayed condition when taken over by the Borough Council in 1966. It was nevertheless of sufficiently good quality to be listed by the Ministry as of architectural and historic interest, and the Council designated part of it as a GIA so that restoration and improvement of the houses and their environment could be carried out with the aid of government grants.

The houses for various grades of employee had been well-built, in stone with slate roofs, to a design that compared very favourably with contemporary mass housing for workers in other parts of the country. The small backyards, each with external lavatory and shed, had become cluttered over the years with various temporary additions. The housing improvement programme included repairs to roofs and defective joinery, adding bathrooms, renewing kitchens and stores and clearing and paving backyards. Environmental improvement included providing garages and parking-spaces for residents and freeing their streets from through traffic and parking by commuters. Unsightly modern lamp standards were replaced by old ones of cast iron. Overhead gas mains (an unusual feature), cables, television aerials and other services were relaid underground. The

61. Swindon: Railway Village (1840s), in process of restoration under GIA procedure.

planting of open spaces with trees, shrubs and grass is already soften-ing the rather hard grid of terraced streets [61]. The renewal as a whole has given great satisfaction to the residents who are at present mostly long-service railway employees; and it will later prove com-mercially viable as a source of desirable rented accommodation close to the new town centre for anyone who may need it.

The GIA policy has clear advantages on several grounds. Socially, it helps to avoid breakdown of communities and kinship groups. Physically, most of the capital originally invested in buildings remains, and only relatively minor expenditure on improvement is required. Administratively, the local authority's costs are kept to a minimum by continued use of existing sewerage, drainage and other piped services, and by its not having to extend refuse collection and other services over greater distances.

Although this policy has kept intact and given new life to town-scapes of 'human' scale, it is open to abuse in some respects. Enhancement of residential areas by restoring the original quality of buildings, improving their surroundings, and using cosmetic treat-ment to make 'nice' areas a bit 'nicer', can sometimes ignore circum-stances of real housing need. It can benefit middle-income groups by letting them take over old districts conveniently near the central area at the expense of the original lower-income residents, who have to move elsewhere – often further from central-area facilities and job opportunities.*

Rehabilitation is, of course, no substitute for building new accom-modation in tune with the times. It has nevertheless made its mark on recent housing programmes, not only by improving the existing stock of housing, but by reminding developers in both public and private sectors of the aversion of ordinary people – 'housing con-sumers' – to tall towers and slabs of 'accommodation units' and 'bedspaces'. By giving continued existence to older dwellings it has increased the nostalgic yearning for houses of human scale: for homes rather than honeycombs.

The necessity for housing at high densities will remain so long as people continue to live in large urban agglomerations and wish to remain within reasonable distances of workplaces and central

*This has been happening, for example, in Barnsbury, North London.

62. *London: Pepys Estate, Deptford: eight-storey and twenty-four-storey blocks of maisonettes (1969–72) and reconditioned 'Terrace' (built 1791). This is part of a 45-acre estate including 3 twenty-four-storey blocks, 10 eight-storey blocks, several four-storey blocks, and a former naval rum warehouse (c. 1780) and coach house providing 65 flats, a library and a sailing centre. Overall density is about 159 persons per acre.*

business districts. As already noted, the prescription for housing in the 1950s and 1960s often produced brutish townscape and inhumane social conditions. There were notable exceptions from sensitive architects with understanding clients: the LCC's Roehampton Estate, Sheffield's Park Hill, Westminster's Lillington Gardens and the GLC's Pepys Estate [62] all make impressive townscape and, as far as can be expected at such high densities, good homes.

Probably the most impressive residential townscape of recent times is nearing completion on the City of London's Barbican site. The then Minister of Housing, Duncan Sandys, recommended in 1956 that this 35-acre bombed site should become 'a genuine residential neighbourhood incorporating schools, shops, open

spaces and other amenities, even if this means forgoing a more remunerative return on the land'. Acceptance of this recommendation brought about a mighty development incorporating 2,113 flats, maisonettes and terrace houses for up to 6,500 residents; a 200-room hostel for students and young City workers; new premises for the City of London School for girls and the Guildhall School of Music and Drama; a theatre, a lending library, an art gallery, a concert hall and a studio cinema to serve residents of Greater London and its surroundings generally; shops, restaurants and pubs, and a completely segregated system of elevated pedestrian walkways and terraces, with motor roads, service access bays and parking for 2,500 private cars located out of sight below pedestrian level.

Housing is concentrated in three towers, each of over 40 storeys (at 412 feet, the highest blocks of flats in Europe), and in multi-storey terrace blocks grouped around squares, courts and gardens. In spite of the high residential density of 230 persons per acre, there are 23 acres of open space for amenity use and 8 acres of lake and planting at ground level. Most of the land has been 'used twice': for example, pedestrian area, building or open space over vehicle access and parking; and pedestrian ways or landscaped terraces over housing and an arts centre, and so on.[4]

The Barbican today is awe-inspiring townscape [63]. It will surely rank among the great architectural and planning achievements of its time, not only for masterly disposition of major elements, but also for sympathetic attention to detail. The City's past is evoked by giving prominence to a stretch of the Roman wall, and to St Giles's Church, once more a lively parish centre; by the felicitous touch of embedding old tombstones in slab seating; and by the occasional use of cast-iron bollards and tall, elegant lamp standards in strongly Victorian tradition. 'Hard' landscaping of paving, ramps, stairs and the lake surrounds is in warm red-brown brick and brick paviors matching those used for walls below the podium level. 'Soft' landscape of grass, trees, shrubs, creepers and stretches of water full of lilies and goldfish is an admirable foil to

◀ *63. London: Barbican; contrasting forms of development with expert attention to detail in floorscape, railings, lamp standards and planting: a pleasant retreat in the heart of the metropolis.*

the buildings, attractive alike to residents and to City workers at leisure. The absence of wheeled traffic confers remarkable tranquillity on so central a location. The presence of schoolchildren and their buzzing activities brings everyday life back to the heart of the City, and tends to reduce the fearsome scale of the buildings. But the Barbican will probably have few imitators. Like Concorde, it proved very costly to build, and it is too costly for most of those for whom it was intended – Londoners of middle and lower-middle income groups.

High-density residential development need not now mean high-rise. The inhumanity associated with giant towers and slabs that, unlike the Barbican, were designed without sensitive relation to other types of dwelling and to local open space has been much reduced in recent housing schemes. Interesting alternatives were sparked off by the ingenious 'Habitat' complex built in 1967 for Montreal's 'Expo'. Here, the main objectives were to take advan-

64. London: Foundling Estate, Bloomsbury, 1971; density about 160 persons per acre.

tage of prefabricated building units and pre-assembled building services, and to give maximum privacy, fresh air, good views and a garden to each dwelling. The prefabricated units, essentially concrete boxes used singly or in twos and threes, made a wide variety of dwellings, most having one roof-garden and some two. Similar ideas are in evidence in the inventive Bishopsfield/Charters Cross scheme at Harlow [2], and in the many variations of stepped 'ziggurat' forms, of which Bloomsbury's Foundling Estate [64] is typical.

Although this scheme attains a density of some 160 persons per net acre, it avoids the sense of isolation felt by families stacked one above another in towers and slabs. The corridor 'streets in the air' serving stepped rows of dwellings, and the shops and other facilities incorporated in large developments such as this, give not only increased privacy for each dwelling but also increased opportunity for people to meet casually and get to know each other. As townscape, housing in this form makes a feature of no mean bulk and somewhat daunting appearance, though far less assertive than tall towers and slabs.

Modern townscape in terms of large-scale extension for typical urban communities is nowhere better illustrated than in British New Towns. The Reith Committee[5] envisaged New Towns as 'an essay in civilisation ... an opportunity to evolve and carry into execution for the benefit of coming generations the means for a happy and gracious way of life'. The later generations that have been living in New Towns for several years would probably not doubt that the Committee's hopes have been largely fulfilled.

Early versions, such as Stevenage, Harlow and Crawley, offered the kind of home in the kind of environment that was the dream of most young families living in overcrowded post-war London, Birmingham, Liverpool, Glasgow and elsewhere. They offered the two-storey family house with garden and garage and 'all mod cons' [65]. More than that, they offered the things that should go with a house : a secure job for the man, a full- or part-time job for the woman, schools, playing fields, parkland, a public library, a health clinic, and central and local shopping centres. Compared with big-city townscapes – tight terraces of three- and four-storey houses, slabs of maisonettes and blocks of flats – the early New Towns were developed at quite low densities, seldom more than 50 persons to the net acre. A variety of types and sizes of house, skilfully arranged along avenues or around small squares, generously 'landscaped' with trees and hedges (preserved or newly planted) and softened by lawns and shrubs, produced as attractive a residential townscape as could be found anywhere in the world for people of comparable income levels. This townscape is now to be seen in matured form in all the early post-war New Towns.

The low-density townscapes had their critics. The sheer numbers of two-storey houses spread over wide areas of land (much of it acquired from private owners in an unfavourable political climate) inevitably appeared monotonous and attracted such epithets as 'more-garden-than-city', 'prairie planning', and so on. In later phases of development in the first batch of New Towns, and in Cumbernauld (c. 1967) and successors such as Runcorn and Milton Keynes, densities as high as 80 persons per net acre were attained. The increase was achieved by building more terraced housing (including the three-storey 'town house' with garage incorporated), 'patio' housing with small yards or gardens, and a slightly higher proportion of flats and maisonettes (though seldom in excess of 5 per cent of all the dwellings); by making gardens smaller generally; and by taking more care to avoid 'SLOAP'.* Increased car ownership also encouraged greater use of the 'Radburn' type of layout, which brought a pleasanter townscape with houses facing on to planted footways and open spaces [65] and wheeled traffic relegated to the rear. Notably sensitive applications of this idea are to be seen in Cumbernauld and Basildon (Laindon 5), as well as in many smaller schemes for the private sector by large firms of builders.

The townscape of central business areas in New Towns proved notably successful and inspired many redevelopments in established towns. Stevenage Town Centre, started in 1956, was the first to secure complete separation of routes of movement for pedestrians and vehicles. With the exception of a few shops around the main bus stop, shopping frontages were made accessible only to people on foot [43]; but every shop could be reached by service vehicles at the rear. In Harlow's centre the Market Place was, at first, separated

* See p. 115.

65. *Stevenage: residential area in the Fairlands neighbourhood, late 1960s. Houses face on to footpaths and open spaces; there is access for vehicles to courtyard garages at rear.*

from Broad Walk by a traffic road; this was later closed to eliminate conflict between pedestrians and vehicles. Most other first-phase New Towns started off with layouts that admitted wheeled traffic to shopping frontages, but later adapted them as pedestrian precincts. By contrast, for various good reasons, the traditional form of a shopping street carrying wheeled traffic was adopted for Hemel Hempstead and, in consequence, the environment for shoppers is less pleasant and less safe than in its contemporaries.

Ambitious ideas for town-centre layout were brought to fruition in 1967 in the fifteenth British New Town, Cumbernauld, in Scotland. A huge multi-level structure in concrete, with decks above a dual-carriageway urban motorway, brought shops, offices, hotel, cinema, dance hall, swimming baths, sports centre, library and civic buildings all under one roof. Parallel decked structures on either side of the motorway are linked by bridges at various intervals and levels. Ground-level space is reserved exclusively for transport and servicing, with routes for buses, cars and vans to get to bus stops, car parks (eventual capacity 5000) and service areas. Escalators and lifts convey shoppers, shop and office workers, hotel patrons and employees and others, to upper floors. Shoppers arriving on foot from their homes enter at first- or second-floor level as ground contours dictate. As this great complex is located on an exposed hill-top, the indoor shopping is appreciated by customers. This satisfactory solution for accommodating many uses in a single multi-level structure has set the tone for similar layouts elsewhere.

Runcorn's 'Shopping City' (opened 1971) is a case in point. The site, in a shallow valley, suggested a decked structure accessible at various levels from a network of pedestrian ways which gravitate from surrounding residential areas and from split-level car parks fed by urban motorways. But this New Town centre has a unique feature: it is at the heart of a public transport system designed as a vital component of circulation for the town as a whole. The Runcorn Busway, as a concept, deserves to rival the fame of the Transporter Bridge of affectionate memory. It seeks to attract as many passengers as possible to use it for travel from their homes to Shopping City, to industrial areas around the periphery, or to other parts of the town. Its buses move along exclusive routes which give fast and unobstructed flow, and arrive at Shopping City on elevated carriageways, whence passengers are set down and collected at main shopping-floor level.

As townscape, Shopping City appears as a massive, rigidly symmetrical concrete structure, punctuated with service towers reminiscent of watch-towers in a medieval town wall, and edged at east and west with stacked car parks. It is not a work of art and was not intended to be; it looks like what it is, a logical container for a complex of everyday activity, and it promises to work efficiently and well.

7: Control and policy for townscapes

Planning control over the development and protection of the physical environment is effected in five principal ways: the preparation and review of development plans (since 1968, structure and local plans); special arrangements for the building of new towns and the expansion of existing towns; arrangements for compulsory purchase and the comprehensive redevelopment of land; the designation of special areas of land such as National Parks, Areas of Outstanding Natural Beauty and Conservation Areas; and the listing of buildings of special architectural or historic interest to give them additional protection.

Local planning authorities exercise control over townscapes through their general control of 'development' under the Town and Country Planning Acts, through their powers relating to outdoor advertisements, and, as already noted, in relation to preservation and conservation. They may also create new townscape by initiating the development of housing, schools and public buildings, and by influencing the routes and designs for new urban roads, including the design and siting of street furniture.

General control stems from the provision of the Town and Country Planning Acts that all development (with very minor exceptions) requires planning permission. Plans for development must be submitted to the local planning authority; if the proposals do not appear to be acceptable in the aesthetic sense, as well as in other respects, they may be rejected or modified. This procedure, though apparently sound in theory, encounters many problems in practice. These include the difficulty of defining the phrase 'acceptable in the aesthetic sense', which has a strongly subjective aspect; the fact that much 'council' building development is subject to continual pressure for economy and is thus liable to skimped standards of 'finish', both in buildings and environmental quality; that proposals from private applicants are often prepared and submitted by persons with no recognized qualifications in design and may be examined by planning authorities, at district level especially, whose officers lack the requisite training and experience to give advice or decisions in design matters; and the fact that departments of government and quasi-government bodies are able to evade planning control, and can often get away with inferior design or building materials in relation to the landscape or townscape in question. But dominating all these is the sheer volume of work entailed in detailed examination by planning staffs of the huge number of planning applications received each year for decision. The Dobry Report[1] states that the average annual number of decisions made by local planning authorities in England and Wales during the 1960s was 428,895; for 1972 and 1973 it was approximately 615,000 and 623,000 respectively. Although the figure will be smaller for 1974 and 1975, it is unlikely that it will be less than 400,000 in years to come. The proportion of refusals is around 15–20 per cent.

When building plans submitted by private developers comply with building regulations, planning committees are reluctant to reject them merely because the designs are unscholarly or dull. Some members of the committee may consider them to be satisfactory; and planning officers who are not trained as architects may share such views or, at any rate, not oppose them so strongly as to press for rejection, especially when lay members of the committee regard the designs as 'just what the public wants'. Uninspiring and hackneyed submissions thus have a better chance of approval than the imaginative and unconventional. A builder or developer who submits unusual designs for planning approval runs the risk of their being rejected, returned for amendment, or delayed while owners in the immediate vicinity are consulted. This causes uncertainty and delay, and probably some financial loss. It is much easier for the developer to submit designs which have received planning consent on previous applications; why should he bother to try out new ideas?

Local planning authorities which do not have staff of sufficient architectural expertise and wish to raise standards of design in their localities may consult advisory panels composed of architects, builders, members of the Council for the Protection of Rural England and others. Such panels, which have been in operation since 1928, are set up by local authorities. They may offer good and imaginative advice in criticizing inadequate designs, but they cannot effect positive improvement short of preparing alternative drawings, which is not their function. Moreover, although the planning committee may seek the panel's advice, it need not take it if it doesn't like it. Frequent changes in the membership of such panels may result in frequent changes of policy, which makes it difficult for developers to know what the planning committee regards as acceptable in various circumstances. On the other hand, infrequent changes of membership may lead to architectural dictatorship.

A planning authority may also employ consultant architects to prepare an architectural framework for particular parts of a town where coordination of new development with existing buildings is especially desirable. In main shopping streets, for example, the framework would indicate such features as canopy lines, cornice lines, window lines and shapes, floor levels, roof slopes, massing on corner sites, and building materials where appropriate. Any new or remodelled buildings would be required to fit into and echo the guidelines. The design and finish would normally reflect the architect's or owner's preferences. For a site of crucial importance the planning authority may appoint a distinguished architect to take sole responsibility for the design, which will also be submitted to the Royal Fine Art Commission for approval. This was the case with the precincts of St Paul's Cathedral, Piccadilly Circus and other key developments in London.

At the root of the general problem, however, is the fact that buildings may still be designed and built by people with no training or qualification in design. Although the figure varies with planning authorities, it is probable that as many as nine out of ten planning applications are submitted by non-architects. The unfortunate consequences of accepting amateur design are very much in evidence, in residential areas especially, and townscapes would stand to gain, though at the expense of a long-enjoyed individual freedom, if the amateur were eliminated. A statutory requirement that no proposal for building development would be considered by a planning authority unless prepared by a suitably qualified person would not assure improvement in the appearance of townscapes, but would increase the chance of achieving it. The 'suitably qualified person' would normally be a chartered architect for new buildings, a chartered building surveyor for conversions or extensions of existing buildings, and a chartered engineer for bridges and other specialist structures.

Where outdoor advertisement is concerned planning authorities are vested with adequate powers of control, but some make more determined use of them than others. Successive Ministers responsible for planning have given consistent support to planning authorities in their efforts to get rid of unsatisfactory advertisements in both town and countryside. Advertisement Regulations prescribed under the Town and Country Planning Acts provide for restricting and controlling the display of outdoor advertisements 'as far as appears expedient in the interests of amenity and public safety', in the cautious ministerial phrase.

The voluntary 'Clutter Code' drawn up by the Advertisers' Association sets standards for advertisements which are not subject to statutory control; these include names and descriptions of activities on shops and other business premises, display notices inside shops or in shop windows and notices put up by public authorities, such as transport timetables. Posters, neon signs, skyline signs and similar displays all require 'express consent', and are controlled by regulations concerning dimensions, appearance, positioning and mode of fixing.

Ugly, brash, outdated or tattered advertisements still spoil the scene in many places, to such an extent that the man in the street may think that little use has been made of powers to control or eliminate them. In fact, very much has been achieved during the past quarter of a century. Of many hundreds of new advertisements considered on appeal each year, some three out of four are rejected. What the man in the street does not see is what townscapes would have looked like in the absence of planning control.

The view is sometimes expressed that rigid control has made British shopping streets less lively than their continental counterparts and that, to enable the scene to be enlivened with more ephemeral spontaneous displays, including pop art, control should be lifted altogether from main shopping streets, apart from those in conservation areas. Such action would probably not be advantageous in a street where drivers of vehicles could have their attention distracted from the road; but it could well be tried in pedestrian-only streets, such as the modified Carnaby Street in London, where the law of marginal utility would eventually operate to keep the size and numbers of advertisements to a lively limit.

It is a manifest disadvantage for townscapes that no effective means has yet been devised to make street furniture an adornment, rather than an eyesore, in the urban scene. Much has been gained by improving the design of individual items; and a little has been gained from the Design Council's valuable lead in recommending new designs for street furniture in a variety of styles and materials.[2] The real problem lies in the fact that while the many authorities and bodies involved – Highway Authority, Post Office, Electricity Boards, parks departments, bus companies, motoring organizations and so on – continue to provide the items for which they alone are responsible, to designs which they alone consider the most appropriate, no single authority has the duty of coordinating the design and siting of the various items as components of the townscape as a whole. It would hardly be reasonable to place the onus on the local planning authorities whose staffs, never plentiful, are already laden with tasks demanding detailed attention and attendance at many meetings. Planning authorities do what they can to secure a measure of coordination, but can hardly become immersed in technical factors of the operation and management of the various services concerned.

In its many successful 'facelift' schemes, the Civic Trust has demonstrated convincingly the kinds of improvement that can be achieved in concerted action under the leadership of an impartial coordinator.[3] The Trust is not able to extend its activities beyond those specific cases in which its consultancy services are engaged. But the point it has made is clear: a special planning service is needed to secure coordination of street impedimenta.

The task might well be entrusted to a new section of the Department of the Environment composed of peripatetic specialist officers who would offer advice and, in difficult cases, work in groups to draw up detailed plans. This proposed section, which might be organized along similar lines to the Planning Inspectorate, would include civil, mechanical and electrical engineers, architects, design consultants and others, with general experience in their basic disciplines and specialist postgraduate training in the visual coordination of street furniture, and with an understanding of the need to conserve the efficiency of each item. Their plans would be drawn up in consultation with local planning authorities and the service authorities and bodies concerned. These plans, once agreed, would be implemented by the local planning authority; in the event of failure to agree, provision would be made for referring plans to the Minister for decision.

The third sphere of planning control over townscapes, namely preservation and conservation, was examined in the previous chapter and needs no further mention here, save to note the advantage to townscapes of extending control over retention or replacement so that it goes beyond individual buildings to groups and settings. This significant change of emphasis from the particular to the general points to the need for further study of the concepts of townscape quality and townscape evaluation and of people's attitudes to changes in townscape.

Quality in townscape is not readily defined; nor is it capable of evaluation in an objective manner. No generally accepted standards have yet been devised whereby alterations or additions to townscapes may be assessed and controlled. It is doubtful whether valid standards could be arrived at, so much depending upon subjective judgements.

Three examples can be cited to illustrate this difficulty. A group of buildings that would be prized in one town might be regarded as almost commonplace in another: Park Square, Leeds, is a rare survival of that city's urbane eighteenth-century town housing, but identical houses in an identical setting in, say, Bath or Dublin would hardly invite a second glance or rank very high among priorities for conservation. A steel-framed glass-clad block of shop-and-office accommodation that might be admired if located in a suburban shopping street would almost certainly be condemned if it arose amid the mature limestone buildings of Chipping Campden or Cirencester.

The visual babel of expensive detached houses of highly individual design which seems cheerfully acceptable in some Belgian seaside resorts would seem hideously discordant in residential areas set aside for private house-building in British New Towns. In each of these examples one observer's view is expressed. Other observers might agree; others again might not. It is the duty of the local planning authority to arrive at development decisions in such cases. On what criteria can their decisions be based?

What people want or expect of their townscape is far from self-evident. The general public can express no unity of preference in matters of taste, any more than in matters of politics or religion. 'Public good taste' is really a fiction (although one cannot but wonder whether this is altogether so, when, for example, crossing the frontier from the messy roadsides of northern Belgium to the neatness of the Netherlands). 'Public opinion' cannot be expected to produce the specific guidance towards criteria that decision-makers need for considering applications to develop or redevelop urban sites. A request to the public at large for an opinion on a particular design for replacement of, or additions to, a familiar building in familiar surroundings* could well elicit from the majority of the few likely to respond a preference for no change at all. This would be symptomatic of the public's increasingly detectable dislike of losing another link with the past and distrust of what may appear in its place.

By what standards of taste, then, must amendments or additions to townscapes be judged on behalf of the general public? Who shall be the arbiters? Shall they be architects, artists, town planners, builders, surveyors, officials advising local planning committees, lay members of such committees, ministry officials? In a democracy the decisions should be an amalgam of as many views as possible; but the consensus view of design is likely to produce a pretty dull compromise. On the comparatively rare occasions when a development can be regarded as a work of art, like a new cathedral, or involves new buildings in close proximity to a work of art, like those surrounding St Paul's Cathedral or the extensions to the Houses of Parliament, the design brief should clearly be entrusted to architects and

*For example, the project to extend the Tate Gallery, London, in the late 1960s.

artists selected by competition and monitored only by the constraints of the financial and other resources available for the project. But, as has been emphasized, townscape is seldom equatable with fine art. It is usually concerned with development for utilitarian purposes, involving considerations not only of architecture but also of town planning, building, estate management and traffic engineering; the final recommendation for decision by the planning committee is usually arrived at by the town planning officer.

This procedure does not leave decisions relating to townscape entirely to the discretion of professional people. Members of the public interested in their town as a whole, as well as the immediate environment of their homes, are showing increasing vigilance over the actions of private developers, local authorities and government and quasi-government departments, and are becoming increasingly involved with decision-making. As individuals, or as local societies, they see the need to examine official intentions and decisions and, where feeling is strong enough, to marshal public opposition to those which they consider objectionable. It is therefore necessary for local planning authorities and others concerned with development to try to discover more about people's attitudes towards their townscape; to become more aware of circumstances in which marked change is likely to be welcomed or resented. And, since people can only express opinions on what they know, it is also necessary to demonstrate what alternatives are available, especially in the context of new forms for houses and flats. These possibilities cannot be made known if architects with new ideas are continually baulked in their efforts to implement them. Instead of the discouragement, rejection or delay that so often greet the unconventional proposal, more encouragement from planning authorities is needed to facilitate experiment with new forms of design and new materials.

Where specific proposals for a town centre redevelopment involve demolition of parts of the fabric and replacement with buildings and spaces of markedly different style and scale, public opinion is usually sounded by publishing illustrated articles and, in important cases, with the aid of exhibition of plans, models, photographs and diagrams. The exhibition technique has been used for many years in London when vital issues are to be decided, such as those involved in rebuilding the environs of St Paul's Cathedral, or redeveloping Piccadilly Circus or Covent Garden. The City Council of Newcastle upon Tyne introduced its ratepayers to ambitious proposals for city-centre redevelopment with an exhibition arranged in a shop in a prominent central location. Similar exhibitions have been mounted in other cities and towns; but although attracting quite large public attendances they will not be of much value in gauging public reaction unless visitors are given the opportunity to ask questions or state views. Visitors should not be offered a blank sheet on which to record views: a set of objective questions to answer, or statements to comment upon, would be more likely to encourage relevant response.

While it is not difficult to obtain public reaction to specific proposals and alternatives, it is much harder to discover in more general terms how people regard and value their environment. Kevin Lynch[4] explored means of expressing how people recognized their urban environment and understood its organization and coherence. He used the terms 'legibility' and 'environmental image' to illustrate the impressions gained by groups of residents in three US cities in terms of three factors: identity, structure and meaning. Lynch defined the concept of 'imageability' as the quality in a physical object which gives it a high probability of evoking a strong image in any given observer. He regarded the city image as comprising five basic elements: *paths, edges, districts, nodes* and *landmarks*. His data were obtained from two basic sources: a systematic field reconnaissance and interviews with residents.

The field reconnaissance of the selected area was made by a trained observer, who mapped the presence of various elements, their visibility, their image strength or weakness, and their connections, disconnections and other interrelations, and noted any special successes or difficulties in the potential image structure. These were subjective judgements based on the immediate appearance of the elements in the field.

The interviews, conducted with a small sample of residents (30 for one city and only 15 each for the other two) were based on questions which sought, among other things, to discover how residents saw their city, which of its features they thought most distinctive, and

167

Townscapes

which features they used for finding their way about the selected area
or for directing people who asked the way.

The technique was complicated. The field reconnaissance took
three to four days and involved asking many questions of passers-
by. The interviews required about one and a half hours of question
and discussion with each person, so that only a very small cross-
section of the population could be expected to participate. No conclusion could be drawn as to how likely the group images derived
from interviews with such a small sample would be to correspond
with the 'public image' assembled from a much larger and more
representative sample.

Lynch's research, however, has stimulated further academic
studies in perception of the environment. Brian Goodey's valuable
examination[5] of Lynch's and other recent work reveals a growing
interest in, and development of, the subject. But so far it appears that
little work has moved sufficiently far from the abstract and complex
stage to be readily applicable in the realm of planning control over
townscape.

Gordon Cullen's technique of 'Notation'[6] is more explicit and
nearer the stage of practical application to townscape analysis than
Lynch's system. His comprehensive 'Scanner' chart, compiling a wide
range of tangible and intangible factors relevant to the environment,
was later presented in the modified 'H A M S Code', which classified
the planners' sphere of influence into four primary divisions:
humanity, *artefacts*, *mood* and *space*. These were in turn subdivided
under the secondary headings of range, use, behaviour and relationship; nine scales for each combination produced a formidable check-
list of factors for observation. Cullen's own examples of the technique's application to actual and imaginary cases, together with the
experience of planners and others who have tried it out, show it to
be a credible, if complex, method of townscape survey. Although described as 'the observant layman's code for his environment', it seems
to rely heavily upon the skill of trained observers rather than upon
expressions of opinion from the man in the street, and is therefore
not representative of public attitudes.

A joint study[7] by the Civic Trust for the North West and the City
of Liverpool's Department of Environmental Health and Protection

produced a simple method of measuring environmental quality, again in relation to physical conditions rather than public attitudes. The area under review in that study, much less complex than the central business district of a city or town, comprised nine streets of nineteenth-century byelaw type in an inner area of Liverpool. Fifteen separate elements of the environment (including noise, pollution, traffic and litter, as well as buildings, floorscape and street furniture) were identified. Points were allocated in respect of each element, and a final tabulation of results enabled assessment of the environmental quality of any particular street as a whole, and of any individual item within a street.

It was possible to draw useful conclusions from the tabulated scores. One point that emerged was that the quantity of litter was directly related to the state of paving in streets and alleyways: broken paving is difficult to sweep and keep tidy, so the worse the condition of paved areas the more litter they attracted. The points system was uncomplicated, and could be used by surveyors unskilled in architecture or planning, though it lacked the subtleties of Cullen's method. It could doubtless be applied to a more complex survey area, such as a town centre, if additional elements of townscape were included to cover the more complicated land-use patterns.

A pilot survey in Reading (see Appendix I) was designed to investigate some general townscape issues, including people's recognition of urban 'character' and 'identity', and two specific issues of current concern: the continued implementation of a plan (agreed in 1965) for redevelopment of the Market Place, and the threatened demolition of the Town Hall. The plan for the Market Place [66] has entailed the gradual removal of existing buildings, listed and otherwise, and their replacement by concrete structures of uniform elevation. The Town Hall [67] (designed by Alfred Waterhouse and built 1872–5) is being replaced by a new building in another part of the central area.

The survey was in the form of a questionnaire which passers-by in selected streets were invited to answer. Of 771 people approached, 652 made a positive response. The general issues – whether people thought that Reading's central area had 'character' and, if so, with what periods that character was mostly associated – were posed

66. Reading: plan
of market place
and proposals
for redevelopment
approved in 1965

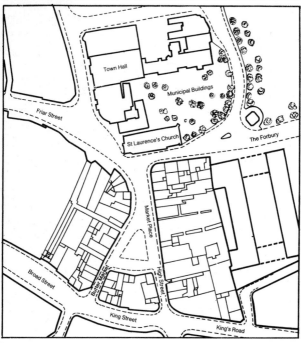

67. *Reading: north end of market place, including a jettied fifteenth-century structure (much restored), a curved early-nineteenth-century block, the Town Hall (by Alfred Waterhouse, 1875) and St Lawrence's Church. Nothing in this scene is safe from demolition.*

by questions framed in relation to six streets, three with predominantly Victorian buildings, two with predominantly Georgian, and one with a mixture of both.

The specific issues were examined by specific questions: Did people know of the existence of the plan for redevelopment of the Market Place? Did they approve of the demolition of the old buildings and the appearance of those put in their place? Did people know that the Town Hall was likely to be demolished? Did they approve? Would they be prepared to make some financial sacrifice for its retention? It is difficult to interpret the findings of such a survey without a measure of personal bias. Nevertheless it can be reasonably inferred that most respondents recognized the town's mature character and heritage of Victorian and other buildings, and showed unwillingness to see that heritage eroded in favour of buildings of the kind recently appearing in the townscape. It can also be inferred that the plan for the Market Place does not now reflect (if it ever did) the preference of a decisive majority of the respondents. The Council's intention not to retain the Town Hall was also disapproved by a clear majority, although the question was at fault in not making clear what 'a little more on the rates' meant. An estimate of the rate-increase needed to keep the building for a new use might have produced an even clearer majority; but a near dead-heat over willingness to pay for its retention is significant, since suggestions of any kind that involve higher rates are rarely welcomed.

Informative though surveys of public opinion may be, they have obvious limitations. It is seldom possible to obtain a response from a sufficient number of people, and from all sectors of the society in question, that is representative of the whole. It is difficult to phrase questions without bias. People unexpectedly stopped in the street and asked to apply their minds to unfamiliar matters of design and planning and to take snap decisions on issues which they might prefer to ponder may be tempted to give hasty answers. Few are likely to have the necessary technical knowledge to appreciate, for example, the consequences of preserving the façade of a building whilst adapting its interior to purposes quite different from those for which it was designed. Nor can people be expected to know the cost-implications of any preferences they may state.

Public opinion cannot produce much more than statements of preference on specific issues – for keeping the old rather than replacing it, for accepting one design solution rather than known alternatives. It could give guidance to designers on such matters as 'open plan' arrangement of housing accommodation versus traditional, or on preference for the 'Radburn' pattern of housing layout fronting footpaths as against the conventional layouts fronting roads. Public opinion cannot, however, take a lead in, or produce ideas for, the creation of townscape; it can only praise or condemn what is there. Architects and planners must obviously take note of known public preferences, but it is their initiative which will present new ideas and new forms to extend the areas of choice.

8: Design control

It has already been emphasized that townscapes cannot be static, but must reflect those changes in urban life and activity which call for and justify new forms of building and spatial development. It is generally accepted, though not by all architects, that planning control should operate to accommodate such changes. Equally, it should operate to resist changes in those parts of the built environment which have architectural or historic merit, or 'group value', worthy of retention.

In the exercise of day-to-day control over development or redevelopment, and for guidance of architects and developers in submitting proposals, it is reasonable to suppose that local planning authorities adopt criteria by which to judge likely changes in visual and other respects. It would not be practicable to devise a single set of design criteria appropriate to the whole range of developments in all towns in a county or all parts of a city or town. Specific standards would be needed to match the character of particular parts of an urban area: a district or 'quarter', a square, a market place, a high street, a secondary shopping street, or even the environment of a single significant building.

Where several new buildings are to be inserted as replacements into an environment containing one or two buildings of outstanding architectural merit, it is reasonable to expect a scale and character in the designs proposed that acknowledge and seek to enhance the setting of their distinguished neighbours without pretending to be of similar period or distinction. In other words, the new buildings should express well-mannered modern designs which respect these outstanding qualities but do not compete with them.

Where only one or two replacements are to go into an environment composed predominantly of buildings of a single characteristic architectural period, the designs should normally conform as closely as possible to the existing majority as regards height, mass, form, materials, colour and general external appearance [68]. Nevertheless, a planning authority should be willing to consider designs for modern buildings which seek to introduce an element of contrast which would enhance rather than detract from the existing environment.

Another set of criteria would be needed where redevelopment in current architectural styles is to follow wholesale demolition of slum, or otherwise uneconomic, properties. It would then be for the local planning authority to set guide-lines for the development of the area as a whole. For mainly residential development a 'development brief' would specify the density and scale of the accommodation needed, and would refer to such factors as layout of roads and footpaths to segregate routes of movement for pedestrians and vehicles, play-

68. London: Portland Place. Unmannerly insertion of a bulky block of flats (1930s) into an Adam terrace (1775), even shaving off an angle of the pediment and removing one and a half pilasters, as well as rudely interrupting the flow of streetscape.

spaces and open spaces, design of buildings, materials to be used for roofs and walls in particular localities, walls and fences as integral features of the architectural and landscape design, street furniture, tree-planting, and so on. In the case of mainly commercial development, the 'development brief' would be expressed in terms of plot ratio, bulk, scale, uses and character, daylighting, rear access, car-parking, adherence to building lines, and similar factors. Within these constraints, architects or developers tendering for the project would produce their own versions for approval by the planning authority.

Development or redevelopment in town centres in terms of single buildings has often been a speculative venture with no single client–user in mind but affording scope for adapting floorspace to a variety of business activities. As townscape, such development was often as anonymous and impersonal in appearance as it proved to be in use. Moreover, in many cases it failed to provide an arrangement of accommodation that was efficient and convenient for its occupants: this was one of the reasons for the long non-occupation of London's notorious Centre Point building, where, it is claimed, the 4,300 square feet of space on each floor is insufficient to house the departments of a large modern business undertaking. A further visual disadvantage of impersonal, speculative, shop-and-office development may become evident when a single large building is erected on two or more adjacent plots amalgamated for the purpose [54]. Whereas the traditional pattern of buildings erected on narrow plots at different times shows a distinctive vertical accent, a new single building, such as New Zealand House [69] in the Haymarket, London, its deep fascia with a long podium extending over several amalgamated plot-frontages, can introduce a strong and alien horizontal accent to the street as a whole, as well as an alien vertical accent in the surrounding townscape.

The tendency is, however, increasing for buildings to be designed and built for a client's specific requirements, and this affords opportunity for the architect to express the purpose and personality in the composition. As the traditional urban central area is essentially an aggregation of specialized buildings, modern townscapes are likely to benefit more from the 'one-off', purpose-built structure than from

69. London: New Zealand House, Haymarket, 1963: impressive and well-detailed office block, unfortunately sited in a townscape of good Edwardian and earlier buildings which have many years of useful life in them.

Townscapes

the speculative all-purpose block. In designing special-user buildings architects clearly need the maximum latitude to express their ideas, consistent with the observance of plot ratio, daylighting and other standards for the locality.

Silhouette is another element of townscape that needs strong control for its protection and enhancement. The typical medieval silhouette of soaring spires and steep-pitched roofs, which Pugin tried to preserve or re-create,[1] can still be observed almost unchanged from a distance in a few small towns, but has almost disappeared from major cities and towns. Some of the quality of earlier silhouettes is not altogether lost, however, because some of the buildings that created it – the cathedrals, churches, town halls and so on – still survive as strong visual accents within the ancient core. Skylines of quite different forms emerging from Georgian, Victorian and Edwardian urban developments have been dominated, often brutally, by the towers and slabs of recent years.*

Some famous silhouettes call for very firm protection because they are being overwhelmed and spoiled by modern development. For example, the skyline of towers, flèches and turrets of the Palace of Westminster, seen from the north-west corner of Parliament Square and from some standpoints south of the Thames, is still as impressive and uncluttered as when it was completed; but from other viewpoints, notably the South Bank complex[2] [70], alien elements impinge upon foreground and background.

Uncontrolled siting of high buildings could greatly reduce the magic or majesty of skylines. The Greater London Council seeks to prevent or halt such damage by specifying in the *GLDP Report of Studies*[3] a series of areas of 'Metropolitan importance', with a subsection on high buildings which defines three categories of area: (i) in which high buildings are inappropriate; (ii) which are particularly sensitive to the impact of high buildings; and (iii) in which a more flexible or positive approach is possible. Among areas in categories (i) or (ii) are such famous views as the National Gallery from Whitehall, Buckingham Palace from the Mall, Westminster from the Serpentine Bridge, Horse Guards and Whitehall from St James's

* See Chapter 4, p. 93–6.

178

70. London: the unique skyline of the Palace of Westminster invaded by clumsy cuboids in the background; they are also visible from ground level.

Park and St Paul's from Westminster Pier. A series of maps entitled 'Sensitivity to High Buildings' (reproduced diagrammatically in figure 8.15 of the *Report of Studies*) shows in broad terms the areas to which the three categories apply. They are not statutory, but are intended to guide London borough councils in the detailed definition of areas on their local development plans.

These proposals came too late to prevent the grave impairment of views by brutish high buildings constructed in recent years. Late, also, is the policy to be adopted for the City of London's Conservation Area No. 6, which includes the Bank of England, Mansion House and the Royal Exchange. This policy 'seeks to preserve the historically significant street pattern, well-known views and general character of this national set piece. High buildings are unlikely to be approved in this area'. In some instances, notably the present background of the Bank of England and Royal Exchange seen from the Mansion House [45], it now seems hardly worth closing the stable door.

71. *Dublin: St Stephen's Green: elegant Georgian terrace with modern insertions which at least observe height limits. But why the coarse concrete canopy (near centre)?*

New buildings, high or otherwise, which take their places in an established street or square should make a positive contribution to the existing qualities of balance, continuity and cohesion in the environment. Such a contribution ought to be possible if the planning authority knows what it wants, and if it succeeds in communicating its intentions to prospective developers. Three factors are of crucial importance in this context. The first is the ability of planning authorities to define their requirements for the environment in question, and to prepare such design briefs as may be necessary to explain them. The second is the willingness of developers not to squeeze the last drop of profit from the site by insisting on the maximum of accommodation, but to spare some for incorporating grace and delight in the external appearance of the building. Finally there is the ability and willingness of architects to produce design solutions that represent mannerly additions to the scene, rather than reflecting the 'alone-I-did-it' approach, which achieves notoriety at the cost of belittling neighbouring buildings [69, 71].

The discussion in the last dozen paragraphs has assumed that planning authorities draw up criteria against which to exercise design control over new development. Do such criteria really exist? Preliminary inquiries of several representative planning authorities, metropolitan and county, suggested that they do not, or at least not in precise terms. Further inquiries and discussions revealed that unwritten or unpublicized criteria are, in fact, employed in assisting authorities to arrive at day-to-day decisions. Planning officers seem somewhat uneasy concerning this aspect of their work. The unease stems from the difficulties inherent in defining and enforcing criteria in such a way as to achieve acceptable townscape without meticulous control or the stultifying of originality and progress in design.

In fact there can be no unequivocal standards for design. Standards must vary from city to city, from town to town, from place to place within towns. They must also change to meet developments in size, forms of construction, cladding materials, servicing, daylighting and so on. There can never be a single solution to a design brief: there should be as many possible solutions as there are inventive architects.

Where the enforcement of criteria is concerned, control must be tempered with understanding of the need to leave scope for architects to demonstrate originality in style and methods of construction. The importance of this emerges in George Dobry's Interim Report for the Department of the Environment's Review of the Development Control System:

It is even argued that much that we find admirable in our existing townscapes and elsewhere, and acknowledge as bringing variety and interest to the local scene, is the result of the personal idiosyncrasies of a past age which may well have been controversial, even actively disliked, when they were new. It is certainly true that fashion changes, and it may well be that the styles we admire now will pass out of favour and some of those we reject become more widely liked.[4]

If London's Festival Hall, Hayward Gallery [47], Queen Elizabeth Hall and National Theatre do not evoke admiration or affection among some – possibly the majority – of their visitors, they at least demonstrate new departures in design and construction. The planning

Townscapes

committee that decided to embark upon such unfamiliar and untried forms took a courageous decision. But it unfortunately opened
the way to a stream of poor imitations thrust into unsuitable environments.

What, then, are the criteria used in practice by planning authorities? It is likely that they would consider whether the proposed development –

(1) observes the general mass and height of surrounding buildings (68 does not);
(2) accords with the materials and colours used for surrounding
buildings, including roofs if visible, especially if these materials
and colours afford a strong unifying element in the street or
square as a composition (71 does not);
(3) is of such a markedly contrasting form as to represent a very
discordant component in the immediate area (as 69 is);
(4) has windows, doorcases and other features in elevations that
relate satisfactorily to those in adjacent buildings (72 does not);
(5) introduces a pitched roof into a street of predominantly flat-
roofed and parapet buildings, or vice versa, so as to cause dis-
ruption in the general appearance;
(6) matches the spirit of surrounding buildings in being, for
example, formal, refined, sober, colourful, airy, or even garish.

Criteria such as these give guide-lines which leave the planning
authority with a desirable degree of flexibility when assessing each
application for new development or redevelopment. To be free to
exercise discretion is far preferable to being tied to codified standards, which tend towards the unimaginative rigidity of byelaw
control. Of crucial importance is the need to brief architects and their
clients before they become committed to a particular design for their
project. Frustration and waste of time can be avoided if consultation
takes place between the developers and the planning authority at
all stages. Detailed discussions of plans and visits to the site are indispensable for major projects on key sites. However, usefulness of such
discussions and the ultimate success of the project rest very largely
upon the quality of the architect's work. A good design cannot easily
be improved; a poor design cannot usually be improved at all.

If planning authorities generally show reticence in publicizing criteria for day-to-day control over the aesthetics of development, they seem more forthcoming and positive in relation to development in conservation areas. Increasingly, policy statements and guide-lines are being published for the information of architects and developers. Some are concerned with particular areas, others with general issues.

Westminster City Council has published two helpful documents: 'Conservation in Westminster'[5] and 'Maida Vale Conservation'.[6] The first, which defines nineteen areas, includes an explanation of the term 'character' as 'the sum of the qualities that make up the individuality of an area; the means whereby the area is recognized as different from others; an amalgam of the area's most distinguished features'. The criteria recommended are broadly similar to those set out above;* but three specific additions are that –

* See p. 182.

72. *Northampton: No. 39 St Giles Street. The alterations to fascia, columns and basement, in alien style, size and materials, imposed on this mannerly mid-Victorian shop, originally similar to Nos. 35, 37 and 41, detract from the unity and dignity of the group.*

'designers of new buildings will be required to re-create the narrow-ings or widenings of streets, and the points of punctuation, where these are characteristic components of the townscape';

'where amalgamation of sites for redevelopment leads to proposals which are out of scale with their surroundings, the façades may be broken down into smaller parts, each of which is in scale with the area';

'simple robustness in detail will commend itself where design demands it, but will not be accepted as an excuse for crudity'.

Westminster's draft policy-paper for Maida Vale includes criteria for new development, supported by drawings to indicate the kind of treatment recommended for insertion of new buildings into existing terraces or of free-standing replacements into streets of villas. Attention is also drawn to the detailed treatment of paving, coal-hole covers, street lamps, boundary walls and fences, shop-fronts, shop and hotel signs, and trees.

Another London borough has prepared draft guide-lines for a long-established village within its area which has been declared a conservation area. Of particular interest is the section on old shop-fronts. Long-established traders are tending to be replaced by chain retailers or trendy boutiques. Chain retailers offend traditional local identity by imposing the standard-lettering fascias and window details which they use in every high street in the country. Established traders also offend by succumbing to the trend towards diversity of design ideas in order to project a stylistic image of their merchandise. Although the trendy design may prove uncongenial, it will probably be less so than the dull standardization of the chain stores.

While eschewing rigid design criteria for new development, this borough has set quite clear guide-lines which developers are expected to observe:

(1) The standard 'corporate identity' shop-front will be discouraged.

(2) The use of mill-finished aluminium standard shop-fronts will be discouraged. Where aluminium is used, it should be anodized bronze or brown.

73. *Tewkesbury: buildings of sixteenth and eighteenth century gutted at ground floor and 'floating' on a bland fascia, though with some attempt made to carry support visually from ground to upper floors.*

(3) Whenever a developer is combining two or more units into one, each unit should be treated as though it were still in individual tenure. The fascia should not necessarily line through between the two units, and lettering of different type face should be applied to each. Stepping of the building on slopes should be accentuated rather than blurred by the shop-front. The effect of non-observance is seen in 73.

(4) The use of traditional design styles in inappropriate contexts, e.g. Georgian shop-fronts in Edwardian buildings, will be discouraged.

(5) The use of traditional local materials such as brick, tiles, timber or slate is preferable to marble, metals, stone, mosaics or plastics.

(6) The retention of pilasters dividing fronts vertically and string

courses or cornices dividing fronts from the building above is important. Often the loss of these features tends to blur the distinction between shop and the rest of the building.

(7) Generally, three-dimensional modelling of the shop-front will be encouraged.

The wording used in these guide-lines – 'discouraged', 'should be treated', and so on – is significant. As legislation now stands, planning authorities cannot prevent a developer from making alterations to his building which are at variance with their ideas. At most, they may advise against, or delay approval of, proposals for such alterations; but, if they refuse planning permission for 'development' which accords with the building regulations, the developer might well get the refusal reversed on appeal to the Minister.

Planning authorities' exercise of control over the external appearance of buildings has rankled with many architects over many years. Architects resent criticism of their work by planning authorities, especially by those whose staff may lack equivalent design expertise, or whose notions as to what is good, bad or suitable in a particular instance are not clearly demonstrable or justifiable. Architects regard their years of training and experience as entitling them to a freedom from lay criticism similar to that normally accorded to physicians or surgeons. They also contend that, even if a planning authority has advice from architects in its employ or from advisory panels, its office is in practice so overwhelmed with applications as to be unable to examine each one with the care it deserves. But perhaps their strongest assertion is that official interference with design kills creativity and discourages any but 'safe', standard responses to design challenges, leading to dull uniformity in townscapes.

This controversy is of long standing, and need not be examined at length here. That architects' designs should be considered only by their professional 'equals' ought not to be in dispute. The vital issues are, on the one hand, whether the time and effort of planning officials should be spent in examining and improving proposals submitted by people with no formal qualification in architectural design, and, on the other, whether similarly unqualified officials should influence design decisions in the planning office. Ideally, in either case the answer should be no. Nevertheless, so long as planning authorities are required to consider applications from unqualified agents and are without sufficient qualified architectural staff, the present unsatisfactory conditions will continue. In his Final Report to the Department of the Environment on development control, George Dobry[7] considered that aesthetic control by planning authorities should remain. Among his reasons were that such control can be a positive planning tool which can objectively improve a development proposal; that some design proposals are visually illiterate and need to be prevented or improved; and that architectural qualifications by no means guarantee that their holder will always produce, even in aesthetic terms, an acceptable design.

9: Some examples of conservation

A crucial issue for townscape is the extent to which planning control succeeds in preventing significant change in the character of some parts of a town whilst encouraging change in other parts of entirely different scale, density and layout. Some towns developed so rapidly during the nineteenth century that their pre-nineteenth-century character has all but disappeared; their inherited medieval or Georgian fabric may be so meagre and in such a state of neglect as to make only a few buildings worth keeping. In such cases redevelopment will accord with modern planning standards and modern architectural styles, unhampered by the physical constraints of past ages. Other towns which, like Alfriston and Warwick, have retained much of the maturity and delight of earlier centuries or, like Bath and New Alresford, consist essentially of large areas developed in one distinguished period, demand as little change as possible in buildings or fabric. But the issue is seldom presented in terms of such clear alternatives. Most towns have some streets or places or 'quarters' (small districts) which are, or could again become, so evocative of historic stages of growth as to make their continued existence, in good repair and beneficial use, indispensable to the town's special identity.

The issue is not merely one of identity, however. Restoration and rehabilitation of buildings in old streets, places or quarters has the advantage of making profitable use of land near the central area. It can bring more people to live and work once more in an old and hitherto neglected part of the town. It can house them in mature buildings adapted to modern standards of hygiene and convenience. It can reinstate exclusively for pedestrians an arrangement of streets and paths originally used by pedestrians and later abused by vehicles. It brings enhancement of land and building values, as well as increasing rate-income for the local authority; and, if a greater number of people are accommodated in the buildings after rehabilitation than before, it will contribute towards decreasing journeys to work and checking the spread of new housing in suburban districts.

Restoration and rehabilitation can, however, release less beneficial influences. Temptingly high profits can accrue from increasing the supply and quality of accommodation in newly fashionable districts close to town centres, especially if rehabilitated properties are to be occupied by people of higher income than formerly lived there. If some residents are reluctant to leave, thereby baulking these prospects of profit, pressure and even harassment may result. Rehabilitation – 'gentrification', as it is sometimes called – can damage the social fabric. It can lead to displacement, dispersal and even total loss of small businesses, such as tailors, dressmakers, boot repairers, jobbing carpenters, second-hand shops and low-price restaurants, which have operated in the district for many years. This may mean the break-up of an intricate pattern of community life and of interdependence among small firms that have worked with each other over generations, as well as serving their clientele both locally and beyond the boundaries of the town.

Such a disintegration occurred as a consequence of the rapid development of London's Carnaby Street from a back-street service and residential area to a popular shopping mall. A similar breakup on a larger scale is threatened in the Covent Garden area following the departure of the wholesale market to Nine Elms. But it may equally well be the case that occupiers of sub-standard accommodation in old quarters welcome a chance to move to clean, well-heated, roomier (and possibly subsidized) accommodation in the suburbs, near to schools and other social facilities, and possibly within short travelling distance of jobs in industrial or other employment.

A local authority wishing to initiate conservation, improvement and rehabilitation in a part of its town may use 'Action Area', 'General Improvement Area' or 'face-lift' procedures. In any case, it can start by setting an example to property-owners in the area. (That is, if the process has not already been set in motion by a property developer who has seen the potential profit and grasped the opportunity.) The local authority can use properties which it owns, or can acquire properties (preferably by agreement), for restoration and adaptation to new uses so as to demonstrate the practical possibilities and financial viability of the venture. Initiative of this kind has stimulated individual owners to participate, but several owners acting independently and at different times seldom succeed in producing a satisfactory environment. A plan is essential as a means of matching each new or improved building to the fabric and ensuring that the environment as a whole is brought up to good standards.

The plan must be drawn up by or for the local planning authority in consultation with all owners, and discussed with and approved by as many of them as possible. The first consideration is likely to be the future control of traffic. A traffic plan would normally include proposals for closing off 'through traffic' routes and eliminating accident 'black spots', providing routes of travel for the exclusive use of either pedestrians or vehicles and any additional routes needed for both, providing garaging and parking space for residents and visitors, and getting rid of all-day parking by commuters and other non-residents. The plan might also provide for reduction of carriageway-width in some streets to allow wider pavements and possibly give space for sloping, instead of vertical, retaining walls to give more light to basements. Over-long back gardens, or back land used for such purposes as builders' yards or scrap-yards, might prove suitable for garaging, parking, playspace and amenity open space, or additional housing.

The plan would be accompanied by a written statement giving guide-lines for such matters as the restoration of elevations (including details for doors, fanlights, windows and iron-work on balconies and railings), colour-schemes, and building materials to be used for repairs to façades and roofs or for extension or rebuilding. It might also refer to the rearrangement and replacement of street furniture (especially street lighting), repair of paving, additional tree-planting and general tidying-up. But, above all, the plan must recognize the fact that restoration of authentic external appearance should not be the only objective. Restoration should start from the inside. The grace and delight of a well-restored exterior should reflect an interior of well-planned accommodation.

The many successful 'face-lift' schemes devised and implemented under the guidance of the Civic Trust demonstrate admirably how conservation projects which are more than skin-deep may be launched and managed.[1] The keynote to success is always a plan that inspires confidence and encourages cooperative action by willing owners, especially when most of them wish to go on living or working in their own premises or in the locality.

An important point needs to be stressed, however. General planning powers over development may be used to control the height, bulk and external appearance of new buildings. They also operate to control change of use and major alterations to the external appearance of buildings to be rehabilitated; indirectly, they may help to retain the small units of accommodation for shops, offices or housing typical of the locality in question. But these powers cannot be extended to control internal alterations to buildings, including amalgamation into larger units. And, even if a satisfactory retention of small units is achieved, planning powers are not available to control the rents which private developers may ask for such units after rehabilitation. Developers will want to charge what the market will bear, and this may well be beyond the means of former tenants. The only way of ensuring that former tenants can continue to work and live in the remodelled buildings is for the local authority to acquire the properties, implement the scheme of conservation and redevelopment and manage the premises as landlord. This would probably entail subsidies from the rates, and the local council would have to consider whether such a policy was justifiable.

Let us now look at some examples of conservation in practice.

Faversham's Abbey Street scheme,[2] an early conservation enterprise, was conceived at a time when most councils and rate-payers saw housing policy in terms of clearance and rebuilding rather than restoration and renewal. By 1957 this historic and potentially delightful street, comprising mostly medieval timber-framed structures overlaid with elevations of eighteenth- and nineteenth-century date, had become so shabby and was deteriorating so rapidly as to qualify for wholesale demolition and rebuilding. Most townspeople regarded it as a slum; most occupiers of premises there hoped to move to new houses on the outskirts of the town; most owners saw no point in spending anything but the minimum on maintenance; one owner-occupier kept chickens in the attic.

A report prepared by the Society for the Protection of Ancient Buildings at the request of the borough council drew attention to the merits of buildings in Abbey Street, both as individual components and collectively as a street scene. It noted that all buildings were capable of restoration at a cost less than that of demolition and building anew.

With the intention of stimulating interest in restoration and re-habilitation among private owners, the council acquired a few properties: the happy results achieved set the example for further effort. Although the declared policy was one of preservation and restoration by 'responsible ownership' rather than 'municipal ownership', the council agreed to acquire as many properties as the rate-income of a small borough of 14,000 ratepayers would allow, and to sell them to private persons under covenant to restore them to the council's satisfaction, with the aid of improvement grants and loans. The success of early restorations led to wider interest among owner-occupiers, several of whom undertook restoration work with the aid of grants from the Historic Buildings Council and the local council. To date, thirty-six houses have been restored and ten await restoration [23].

The setting of these renewed buildings has been much enhanced by the removal of a messy wirescape, narrowing of the carriageway and widening and repaving of footways, and the introduction of a strip of stone setts to cover ducts for street lighting, drainage and other services. Tall, slender lamp standards crowned by quietly elegant lanterns add to the visual pleasure of this satisfying streetscape, but the scene would be further improved if individual television aerials could be replaced by a single aerial to serve all premises in the street.

It is pleasant to record that in the course of this venture in conservation only eight occupiers were displaced from unfit houses; these people were re-housed by the council. No residents were displaced against their will, and no Compulsory Purchase Orders were used. The ambition of most of the former tenants was to obtain a modern council house. Restored premises have tended to be occupied by owners or purchasers in the middle-income group, since a fairly substantial income is needed to cover mortgage repayments and the comparatively high maintenance costs associated with old properties. The residents are predominantly professionals, architects, teachers, journalists and others, who work locally. There are no 'week-enders'.

The venture proved profitable for the council, although profit was not one of the original objectives. It brought back into rating, at increased rateable values, premises that would otherwise have become uninhabitable. It also brought an increase in property values in the street, enabling the council to sell properties at market prices substantially higher than the original costs of acquisition. The capital thus gained helped the council to build eight flats for old people on a surplus area of back land.

Middelburg, a stately old Dutch city which is the capital of Zeeland Province, was badly damaged by bombing during the last war. Until 1961 the Municipal Council, together with private owners of property in the historic core, had concentrated effort on repairing the grievous damage done to major buildings. Subsequently, attention turned to the conservation of areas in the inner ring, where properties suffered not so much from enemy action as from neglect, ill-use or under-use over long periods. These areas have now become attractive for residential resettlement.

The compact, informal fabric of narrow streets, passages and 'places' has scarcely changed since medieval times. Terraced houses on narrow plots show a strong vertical accent, architecturally, and there is a sympathetic relationship between heights of buildings and widths of streets and spaces. Deep plots afford garden space which, for most old Dutch cities, is an unaccustomed luxury. The properties give equally ready access to the city centre, with its noble public buildings, elegant town hall, spacious market place and high-grade shops, and to the pleasing sweep of parkland that replaced the former wide town walls and ramparts. The residential areas are not invaded by heavy and constant vehicular traffic, but enjoy a large measure of silence and repose. These are the enviable qualities which attract people in increasing numbers to take up residence once more in the

old city, and which provided the impetus for conservation and renewal.

The council pursues conservation as an integral part of planning policy. In 1961 there were some 960 small dwellings of architectural or historic interest in the city. Of these, 100 were in near-slum condition and 250 had so deteriorated as to require urgent action for renewal. Over the succeeding eight years the demand for such restored properties proved so strong as to justify the council's embarking upon schemes embracing one or more complete streets at a time. When launching a project to restore houses for sale, such as that for 40 houses in the Spanjaardstraat [74], the council acquires the properties and prepares a plan showing how vehicular access, garages and sheds will be provided for each dwelling. The land needed for this is normally obtained by taking a strip from the end of each garden. The council also has the front gables restored to their former condition in order to re-create an authentic street elevation, and maintains the traditional 'floorscape' of paving and brick-on-edge or setts.

Properties are then sold to individual purchasers, who must covenant to submit plans for redevelopment and to complete the work by an agreed date. Purchasers are eligible for subsidies. Where the cost of restoration does not exceed fl.20,000, these are 25 per cent of the cost from central government and municipal funds and 5 per cent from the provincial government; where the cost does exceed this figure, the contributions are respectively 30 per cent and 10 per cent (with a further 5 per cent of the cost in excess of fl.30,000). The purchaser's contribution would be 70 per cent or 60 per cent (or slightly less) respectively. Each purchaser may employ his own architect or may obtain architectural assistance from the council to plan an internal layout to accord with his household's particular wishes.

Specimen figures published by the council[3] in respect of houses in the Spanjaardstraat show that restoration costs for a house of 421 cubic metres were fl.151,883, but subsidies of fl.85,895 gave

74. *Middelburg: Spanjaardstraat: house at right built in 1608, others of seventeenth- and eighteenth-century dates; 'footscape' being restored; garages and parking space at rear of rehabilitated houses.*

195

a net cost to owner of fl.66,288; for a house of 590 cubic metres the figures were fl.195,385, fl.103,992 and fl.91,393, respectively.

A similar project undertaken by a housing association involved the purchase of 30 houses in the Bellinkstraat which, after restoration by the association, were let at rents of the order of fl.350 per month. Proposals for the restoration of any 'listed' buildings require approval from the municipal council and the Rijksdienst voor Monumentenzorg, which is the equivalent of the British Department of the Environment, Historic Buildings Section.

The council has a long waiting list of applicants for restored properties. Purchasers have not been slow to recognize the benefits of owning a house of mature architectural character, with garden and garage, and accommodation designed to their own requirements, in a quiet district within easy walking distance of the central area and railway station. The smaller properties are tending to be purchased by retired persons, but the larger ones are sought after by families with young children. Houses restored by housing associations are available for small or large households. Schools in the neighbourhood can be expanded as necessary, and there seems no reason why the districts should not in due course have a representative cross-section of the community, including young and old, well-off and less well-off. Visits to several of these restored properties and conversations with their owners leave no doubt as to the satisfaction which this policy of conservation has given to both parties to the transactions. Its continuance will do much to ensure the economic and social survival of this fine old city.

Chur, or Coire, is an ancient Swiss city, capital of the Graubunden (Grisons) canton. Its council recently embarked upon what should prove a model of conservation and rehabilitation, not only for that city but for others of similar character. The project area is an ancient market place in which warehouses built later deprived surrounding tall buildings of sunlight, reducing their value and pleasantness as places to live and work in. The stated objectives of the plan[4] are to retain what is valuable, to re-accentuate and renew what is

75. *Chur: map showing rehabilitation proposals and progress, as at April 1975.* ▶

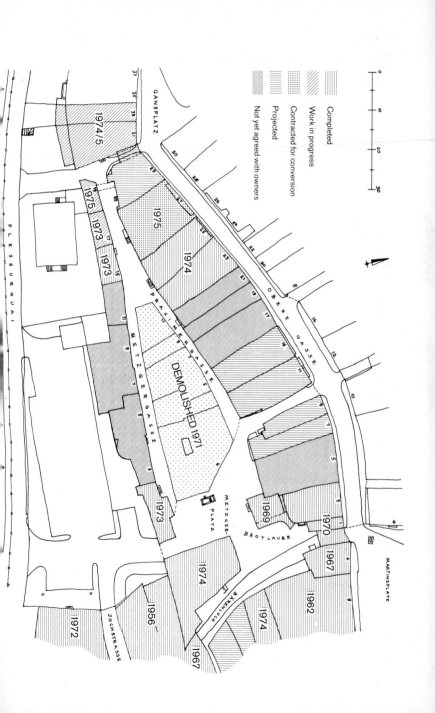

Completed

Work in progress

Contracted for conversion

Projected

Not yet agreed with owners

GANSPLATZ

37

35

33

31

PLESSURQUAI

1974/5

1975 1973

1973

1975

1974

PRAXMERGASSE

METZGERGASSE

DEMOLISHED 1971

1973

METZGER-PLATZ

BROTLAUBE

JOCHSTRASSE

1972

1956

1974

BÄRENLOCH

1974

1967

1969

1970

1967

1962

OBERE GASSE

MARTINSPLATZ

0   10   20   30

76. *Chur: 'Arcas', looking eastwards. Restored houses at top left; the scaffolded building on the right is the restaurant. The cobbles underlying the asphalt surfacing will be exposed.*

Some examples of conservation

characteristic, and to reject and eliminate what is historically, economically and aesthetically worthless. The council took an effective first step towards these objectives in 1971 by acquiring and demolishing the intruding warehouses.

The market place, now called 'Arcas', is triangular in shape [75]. Along the northern side, the Praximergasse, buildings have return frontage to an important shopping street, the Oberegasse. Along the southern side, the Metzgergasse, buildings back on to a public car park adjoining the wide river-bank called the Plessurquai. The short eastern flank [76] is defined by houses fronting a road through the Metzgerplatz linking the Oberegasse and Plessurquai. The western point is a narrow arcade through which access is gained to an important town road. Most of the buildings around the market place date from the sixteenth century. Those along the Praximergasse are Gothic houses of architectural and historic importance. Those fronting the Metzgergasse, built along the former city wall, have been maltreated architecturally; one of them incorporates the former Metzgertor (Butchers' Gate), which has lost the pointed roof shown in old prints of the medieval panorama of Chur.

The plan envisages the restored market place as a public space for use only by pedestrians, whether as an informal meeting place or as a venue for public gatherings and festivals. It will also afford a setting that will greatly enhance the appearance of the surrounding buildings to be restored. The convenient road link on the eastern flank will continue in use for vehicles, but will not conflict with pedestrian routes. Underneath the market place, the plan provides space for 170 cars: 50 spaces for residents' garages and 120 spaces controlled by meters. Space will also be reserved for small storage units to compensate for the demolished warehouses. Access to underground garages, parking and storage units will be via a common ramp. Cellars under houses lining the Praximergasse will be converted for warehouse use, with service links to the new units. Public lavatories will also be provided. Thus, all works underground (which are due for completion in 1976) are planned to be self-financing.

Above ground, the 22 houses around the market place are all worthy of restoration; 10 have been completed [see 76, top left], and 3 more were completed during 1974–5. Only 2 are owned by the council; the remainder are in private hands, and owners of 9 of these have not yet agreed to participate in the plan. Responsibility for restoration rests with owners, who are not entitled to subsidies. A limited company, Marktplatz–Immobilien AG, has been formed to acquire properties by agreement, to restore their elevations and convert the accommodation, in most cases for residential purposes, and to sell the completed units. In one of the completed houses which the council owns, the company has installed central-heating plant to supply all the other buildings, thus saving owners the cost of individual oil tanks and boilers for each property. Any owner may purchase a connection and obtain heating and domestic hot water on payment of an annual charge.

Study of existing and proposed elevations along the Praximergasse[5] shows that only minor works of restoration would be needed to give the façades and roof-lines an authentic appearance. The buildings are narrow-fronted, in some instances only 4–5 metres wide, and generally about 20 metres deep. Thus at ground level there are opportunities to form arcades and extend shops fronting the Oberegasse by opening new shop windows and entrances on to the arcades or directly on to the market place. In restoring the upper floors of adjacent houses it may be preferable, floor levels permitting, to combine the accommodation horizontally rather than vertically. This would give a more convenient arrangement of rooms in flats, and would require only a single staircase. The characteristic vertical accent of narrow single elevations would nevertheless remain unchanged.

Examination of existing and proposed rear elevations along the Metzgergasse[6] (those fronting the Plessurquai) shows that the historic buildings have been roughly treated in the past, especially at roof level. The proposals include designs for restoring the Metzgertor, for additional loft accommodation under the new roof-lines, and for the garage and parking space underneath the market place. The building with five bays approximately in the middle of the row [seen scaffolded in 76] is being converted for use as a restaurant; on one side it will give pleasant views across the river for patrons, and on the other a focus of attraction for the market place.

This project seems to have all the ingredients for success. Every completed improvement would confer substantial additional value on every other building. The only weakness is that all owners may not agree either to make the necessary capital investment or to sell to the Marktplatz–Immobilien AG. But the increase in property values already stimulated by the work accomplished at this early stage should give sufficient incentive for all to participate, even though it may be several years before they decide to do so.

It is too early yet to assess the social implications of this project. The restored premises must attract a level of rents or purchase prices that reflects the expenditure on buying, restoration, rehabilitation, parking spaces and other works, as well as the increase in land values attributable to the project as it progresses. They are thus unlikely to be within the financial means of families living in the present sub-standard accommodation; but few such families would refuse the offer of a modern council house on the outskirts of the town, near to schools as well as factories and offices. The new occupants are therefore likely to be from the middle-income groups: restaurant managers, shopkeepers associated with the tourist industry, professional offices; and in the residential accommodation, households without young children.

Conservation of townscapes in the United States has gained momentum in recent years. The driving forces are, variously, regret for the destruction of buildings that evoked the past and a wish to retain worthwhile survivors, desire to retain individual buildings which express historic stages and styles of architectural achievement, and stimulation of tourist interest, national and international.

Conservation of historic features of the nation's capital, Washington D.C., is taken very seriously. The grandiose Renaissance plan, prepared by Charles L'Enfant in 1791 and gradually implemented throughout the nineteenth century, survived the vandalism committed by mid-nineteenth-century railway engineers in taking lines across the Mall, and did not suffer from the brutal bulk of skyscrapers that has come to overshadow other great American cities in the present century. The White House, the Capitol, the monuments to great presidents, the impressive if clumsy classicism of the government offices along Pennsylvania Avenue and the other features of the central area have not been belittled by towers and slabs. Typical blocks often to fifteen storeys dating from the early twentieth century still show modest proportions, respect for eighteenth-century scale, and affectionate and cheerful detailing of façades and crowning cornices and parapets. Planning control has proved effective in preserving the restrained and stately character.

Comprehensive planning proposals published in 1967[7] include lists of historic landmarks and significant areas put into three categories: those in I must be preserved; those in II should be preserved or restored if possible; those in III should be preserved or restored if practicable. Each category includes public buildings and monuments, religious buildings and monuments, institutional and educational buildings, commercial and industrial buildings, residential buildings, embassies and clubs, and 'places'. The last-named are squares, circles, vistas, parks and other features of the original plan, distinct communities such as Georgetown and Capitol Hill, and 'special streets'. These last include 'Boundary' (edge) streets marking the limits of segments of the city, 'Symbolic' streets which are avenues set aside for major ceremonial functions and pageantry and great axial streets and avenues, 'Movement' streets for large volumes of vehicular traffic, and 'Connective' streets whose primary purpose is to provide pedestrian connections between various sites of community activity. These categories of buildings and places correspond to some extent with British classification under the Civic Amenities and Town and Country Planning Acts; the Washington Comprehensive Plan did not, however, determine the means for preserving them.

Denver, Colorado, is one of many American cities which have recently become conscious of their 'rugged early days of boom and bust'. In 1965 a group of its citizens[8] started a private-enterprise venture for the conservation of eighteen Victorian buildings around Larimer Square, the core of the original settlement founded in 1858 by General Larimer, conqueror of the surrounding territory. The first buildings in brick, taking the place of log cabins, date from the 1860s and occupy the original sites of the city's first bank, theatre, library, post office and stores. In comparison with ebullient British Victorian architecture, Denver's early buildings are ponderous and restrained, though occasionally ornate. They stand on narrow passages and courtyards reminiscent of the City of London's small courts and lanes.

Rehabilitation has been enthusiastic and discreet; sand-blasted and steam-cleaned brickwork, restored wrought-iron railings, balconies, brackets and gas lamps and sympathetic floorscape give an air of truth to the scene but escape being precious. The old theatre is in use again. Small boutiques, booksellers, antique dealers, jewellers, silversmiths and other shops flourish, as do restaurants with names like 'The Sobriety' and 'My Father's Mustache' serving many varieties of food in lively surroundings. The venture has provided an authentic and popular piece of old townscape which draws more than two million visitors annually, Denver citizens and tourists alike. It has also brought additional revenue to the city in property taxes: these have increased eightfold from 1964 to 1974.

Conservation of an old town in an entirely different modern use is well illustrated by Georgetown, high in the Arapaho National Forest Park in the Rocky Mountains. It arose as a mining settlement during the 1858 gold rush, and grew little until the discovery of silver in 1864. Thereafter, rapid expansion and increasing prosperity brought a charter of self-government in 1868. By then it had a fine courthouse, churches, a school, hotels and bars, stores and even an opera house – on the second floor of one of the few three-storey buildings of brick. Until the silver market crashed in 1893 the town prospered with a resident population of a few hundreds but a Saturday-night population that could reach ten thousand, mostly miners from surrounding camps. Fortunes were lavished on building splendid houses, some of which, with antique and nineteenth-century furniture and furnishings, remain as museum-pieces.

In recent times it has become a second-home week-end retreat and a tourist attraction. In summer, coachloads of visitors descend upon it to discover an 'authentic' mining town; in winter it functions as a centre for winter sports. The modern townscape has a spick-and-span quality unknown in its heyday [77]. The buildings, mostly timber-framed and close-boarded with shingle roofs, and sometimes elegant barge-boarding, gleam with paint and gilding; even the refuse bins and fire hydrants shine newer than new. The only authentic untidiness is the tangle of wirescape. The town reverberates with

77. *Georgetown: a former mining town, product of the 1860s Gold Rush. Now a tourist and holiday centre.*

activity upon the arrival of each coachload of tourists, who fill the streets and the bars for a couple of hours; but with their departure the stillness of the museum returns. This conservation has brought new life and prosperity, but a townscape more tidy than true.

Another form of conservation is façade preservation. This entails neither restoration nor rehabilitation, but preservation coupled with redevelopment. In some instances the result achieved is doubly advantageous; in others it is rather suspect. It involves preserving the front elevation of a building or group but rebuilding part or all of the main structure. Streets, squares, crescents, groups and single buildings of special architectural interest may thus continue to display the harmonious unity of the original composition while gaining a more efficient and economic arrangement of accommodation, either for the original use or for changed uses demanded by the market. The increased versatility of these special features of townscape also helps to stave off the threat of demolition and redevelopment.

This method has permitted the retention, to great visual advantage, of many elegant elevations. John Nash's crescents and terraces in the area of London's Regent's Park retain the grandeur of their façades, while the accommodation behind them has been restored, rearranged, enlarged, or in some cases entirely rebuilt. Cumberland Terrace, for example, is now a block of modern flats which, individually, bear little relation to the palatial façade; the Sussex Place terrace is backed by an entirely new structure designed for the London Graduate School of Business Studies; and other Nash terraces and crescents have been similarly re-designed as suites of offices.

In Salisbury, the Old George Mall project involved redevelopment of a large part of a central-area street block or 'chequer' as a 'precinct' shopping centre, making profitable use of back land. Listed buildings along the boundary streets were retained and put to more profitable use. The large gap in the Old George building at ground level [78] makes a rather incongruous entrance to the precinct from the High Street and robs this fine medieval structure (dating from the early fourteenth century) of much of its integrity as a historic building. The damage to townscape is nevertheless not so great as if the whole had been sacrificed. However, the architecture of some of the 'infilled' buildings along the New Canal frontage ranges from bogus medieval to brutal modern.

Saffron Walden's Post Office[9] shows another application of façade preservation. For many years the sales office operated in a Georgian house in the High Street [79] while the sorting office was in unsatisfactory premises some distance away. As the fabric of the Georgian house had deteriorated, the decision was taken to restore the shell but to replan the interior as a modern post office and to accommodate the sorting office at the rear. The cost of this scheme was the loss of a Georgian interior (in very poor condition) and an expenditure 10 per cent greater than would have been needed to provide equivalent floorspace in a new building. The benefits included excellent modern post-office facilities, with a restaurant and clubroom, and an efficient combination of sorting office and post office.

78. *Salisbury: the Old George, leading into the new shopping mall on back land.*

79. Saffron Walden: Georgian town house in the High Street adapted for use as a Post Office, with the sorting office at the rear. Unsympathetic styles for shops on either side.

In townscape terms, a fine familiar feature on a key site more than holds its own with new neighbours.

This method of conservation invites criticism on several counts. Practical difficulties arise in joining new building work to an old façade; the façade itself may not survive the operation, as was dramatically demonstrated by the collapse of Nash's York Terrace at Regent's Park in 1968 during construction of the new building at the rear. In other instances façades were found to be unsafe after demolition of the remainder and had to be dismantled. Developers then began to plead, often successfully, for abandonment of an old façade in favour of an entirely new building. When granting consent for partial demolition a planning authority therefore needs to impose stringent conditions for safeguarding the stability of the parts to be retained.

In the context of retaining historical evidence, the method is of

207

dubious merit: a façade by itself is of little real historic significance. This approach may also be resorted to as a means of avoiding the level of investment that thorough restoration and renewal would warrant, developers instead economizing with a new building of poor quality wearing an ancient or genteel mask. It can also transform a town with buildings of genuine historic interest into a stage-set townscape of hollowed-out history.

It is not easy to decide in what circumstances and to what extent the method should be encouraged. From one viewpoint it affords the means for cordial coexistence of the handsome traditional and the efficient modern. To allow random removal of individual units in compositions such as Bath's Circus, or London's Bedford Square or Dublin's Fitzwilliam Square, and their replacement with others of quite different styles, materials and colours, would make as unfortunate a blemish as a damaged or discoloured tooth in an otherwise happy smile. Yet mediocre and ill-mannered units have recently invaded terraces in Edinburgh's New Town; and more would have interrupted the splendid visual flow of Dublin's St Stephen's Green, had not determined public opinion resisted ruthless redevelopment.

It may equally be argued that if a building or group has reached the end of its useful and economic life it should be replaced with another in tune with the times and providing accommodation that meets the need of the client. Striving to retain the old can be construed as an expression of no confidence in architects' capacity to produce new buildings that enrich rather than offend the townscape.

A further aspect of conservation is the problem of retaining buildings of architectural or historic interest that occupy sites for which they are now clearly unsuitable. These may be sites in an expanding central area which, in the interests of rational town planning, should be redeveloped with modern buildings at much higher density.

The method of conservation by relocation was used quite extensively in Sweden shortly after the last war when city-centre redevelopments, in modern styles and at high densities, necessitated the freeing of key sites occupied by small buildings of architectural or historic value. Many such buildings had been lost in town fires over the centuries and some were lost in the process of redevelopment; but the best of the survivors in the post-war era were dismantled and re-erected on other urban sites, or in open-air museums like that at Skansen near Stockholm. The need for conservation by relocation arose in acute form at Linköping, in Östergötland Province, where a historic urban fabric stood in the way of important expansion of commerce and industry (including the great SAAB motor works). The conflict was resolved by removing the old buildings from central-area sites in Linköping and re-erecting them on an open site at Valla, a few miles to the south-west of the city centre.

Linköping City Council initiated the project by acquiring all the properties in question and carrying out the work of dismantling and repairing them and re-erecting them at Valla. Most of the buildings were of timber-framed construction, so the work involved was not onerous. The first transfer to Valla, in 1951, was the Huitfeld House, an elegant town house built in 1807 and now set in a reproduction of a mid-nineteenth-century garden complete with summer house. The ground floor of the house is used for receptions and the first floor as a private apartment. Some sixty-five buildings have been re-erected since then. The council retains ownership of all buildings, but has let most of them at economic rents to various types of tenant. About a third of the total are in use as shops, post office, bank, restaurants and workshops for craftsmen including a silversmith, a potter, a woodcarver and artists. Another third are in residential use. The remainder are not inhabited but accommodate various kinds of museum.[10]

Wherever possible, buildings are equipped with contemporary furniture and fittings. They are also set out on a pattern of streets, passages and incidental open spaces reminiscent of, though not reproducing, their setting in old Linköping. Houses that originally had spacious gardens have them now: one has been laid out as a typical eighteenth-century herb garden; others are flower gardens in the styles of the eighteenth and nineteenth centuries. Houses with outbuildings formerly used by craftsmen have the same outbuildings for use, if practicable, by similar craftsmen. The urban scene is further enhanced by the use of paving stones and street lamps brought from the old locations.

Although Valla gives an authentic reflection of some three

centuries of urban tradition in Östergötland, it is not merely a museum. It is a place where people live and earn a living in a variety of ways. It has set a precedent, now being followed in several towns in Sweden and Denmark where the cultural and architectural heritage of past centuries is being renewed by self-financing projects in affectionately recreated townscape.

Coventry's central area had a rich legacy of medieval and post-medieval timber-framed buildings of small scale, mostly burghers' houses and halls. Over the centuries most of them were 'modernized' by being encased with brick and plaster, but the original oak frames remained intact. A survey in 1958 revealed that about 100 such buildings in scattered locations had survived wartime bombing; but another survey in 1966 disclosed that redevelopment had reduced that 100 to 34. Evidence of the burghers' city was vanishing; some of the surviving buildings were in various stages of decay and under threat of demolition. The city council therefore decided to preserve the best by removing them and re-erecting them along one shabby little street where several good examples were located. This is Spon Street, half of which now lies within the new inner ring road immediately west of the new and famous shopping precinct.

Spon Street is admirably suited for this purpose since, as stated in the Townscape Scheme for the area,[11] it will provide a place where ancient buildings can be seen –

(a) in their original form;
(b) as modified through time in response to changing use and fashion;
(c) in their traditional relationship with each other along an existing street;
(d) within surroundings suitable to their scale and proportions;
(e) close to the central area, where sympathetic use, e.g. as small shops, meeting places and houses, would socially and to an extent economically justify their retention (the tourist attraction of the street must not be overlooked in assessing the scheme's value to the city as a whole);
(f) astride a comprehensive pedestrian route linking the shopping precinct, Broadgate, the Cathedral and the Lanchester College.

80. Coventry: Spon Street: at right No. 169, restored; at left Nos. 163–5, the three-storey structure re-erected. Intervening buildings of medieval timber-framed construction are due for restoration.

The present situation of Spon Street is as follows: number 169, a late-fourteenth-century two-bay building, has been restored *in situ* (80); other houses earmarked for retention in the street are in sufficiently good condition and use not to demand immediate attention. The former number 7 Much Park Street now stands, occupied, as number 9 Spon Street. As the consultant architect noted, 'this re-erected building is the first to introduce into Spon Street the sense of scale and quality the City must have possessed in the Middle Ages'.[12] Numbers 8 and 10 Much Park Street, recently erected as numbers 163 to 165 Spon Street [80], represent the only surviving three-storey jettied buildings in Coventry apart from those in Priory Row. Some buildings from other streets have been dismantled and their timbers put in storage for future re-erection. The work of removal, treatment of timbers and re-erection is going slowly, and the 'new–old' Spon Street will take a long time to complete. The council has had no difficulty in letting restored properties as shops. The rents received reflect open-market values and, although they do not at present cover the costs of restoration and re-erection, they may well do so in the future.

Again the question arises of the historic validity of this kind of conservation; but the case for it seems stronger than for façade preservation. The essential feature for conservation – the original element in the structure – is the timber frame, and it was not uncommon for medieval owners of such buildings to dismantle them and re-erect them elsewhere. As the consultant architect emphasized:

The character of the building is once and for all determined by its primary structure and form ... The secondary elements such as stairs, windows and doors may emulate the original (if there were any) in terms of the essence of vernacular design, but on no account must they reproduce examples of the period. Similarly materials, including the timber for repairs or replacements, must be new. The use of any members or fittings obtained from elsewhere regardless of age or design is to introduce fake and deception.

Within these severe limits, the building must be designed, as any other, up to today's standards of heating, insulation, lighting, ventilation and sanitation. Also, as any other, the building operations must be capable of being competitively estimated and then controlled from start to finish. The contract documents are thus quantitatively no different from those of a normal project. Qualitatively, oak technique assumes the major part of the details and the specification.[13]

Such a policy for timber-framed structures will safeguard their integrity, ensure their continued use and reproduce reasonably authentic townscape for both citizens and tourists. Relocation of brick or stone structures, although obviously less practicable, has succeeded in a few cases: a Wren church from London did cross the Atlantic for re-assembly in Fulton, Missouri!

10: Future townscapes

Thoughts about the future of townscape lead to difficult questions to which few answers are forthcoming. What is the optimum size for a city or town, especially one with a core of architectural or historic importance? If urban populations continue to increase, stimulating demands upon central-area land for more shops, offices and administrative and other services, where should the necessary additional urban capacity be located: in existing cities, by new development on the periphery or redevelopment at higher densities of 'inner rings'; or in New Towns; or in small towns, through schemes under the Town Development Acts? If existing cities or towns were expanded, it is likely that their historic centres would not for long withstand pressures for redevelopment at higher densities; individual redevelopments would consist of tall and bulky buildings that would dominate and eventually take over the scene.

How much taller and bulkier are buildings to become? Are blocks of twenty to forty storeys, or even more, to become the norm in city centres? If so, by what criteria will their location be determined and controlled in the interests of townscape? And what of the continuing increase of traffic in towns: will movement of people in private cars, and of goods in lorries of increasing size and number, continue in cities, or will significant restrictions be placed on vehicles' right of access to urban roads, with public transport playing a much greater part? These questions are not readily answered; but until solutions emerge it is hardly possible for clear objectives for townscape to be formulated.

Another question: should the fact of owning land necessarily entitle someone to change the built environment to his own liking and for his own benefit? The planning authority can prescribe conditions for consent to redevelopment, but it cannot question the owner's right to redevelop, except in the case of a listed building or of an unlisted building in a Conservation Area. Should 'society', the general public, the ratepayers, have a stronger voice in consenting or objecting to drastic changes in the appearance of their city or town proposed by a developer acting only in his own interest? Should the present planning controls relating to use, bulk, height, daylighting and external appearance be augmented so that a developer must show cause why his present building should no longer form part of the townscape, and why the one he seeks to erect in its place would bring greater benefit, visual and otherwise, to the urban community as well as to himself?

On the other hand, should ownership of a listed building, or of an unlisted building in a Conservation Area, penalize the particular owner by preventing him from realizing the potential value of his site because the building standing on it gives visual pleasure to the public at large, or makes a good subject for a tourist's camera? Should the owner be further penalized by having to meet from his own pocket the high costs of maintaining an old building in good use and repair, when a modern, purpose-designed one would incur less expense? The law relating to conservation treats such an owner with some severity: it makes no provision for him to be consulted before his building is listed, or for compensation for loss of potential development value or for higher maintenance costs. The law-makers may have asked, but do not seem to have pursued, the question: who are the beneficiaries of conservation, and at whose cost do they enjoy the benefit?

A further question: must all urban development or redevelopment, whether private or public, be undertaken for the maximum profit? Redevelopment in the post-war period has increasingly become a process whereby a few 'big men' drive many 'small men' out of city centres, usually with the tacit approval of planning committees. High streets and market places have been changed out of all recognition, with larger and larger multiples, supermarkets and other retail units, and fewer and fewer small businesses. This is more intensive and efficient use of central-area land, and can be justified in economic terms. But how far should the economic argument be taken in the case of a city with a central core of architectural or historic interest?

And, perhaps equally important, how far must the process extend into pockets of lower-value land adjoining the central core? Would cities and towns not be more human, more lively, more interesting if work-places and homes kept a balance between new and old, shiny and shabby, luxurious and spartan?

There is surely a case for modest, as well as prestigious, standards for city-centre development: for business premises without impressive entrance halls, without underfloor heating and lifts, without garages for principals' cars and without porters and commissionaires, but with accommodation at rents to suit small businesses and rising young professionals. There is also a continuing need for reasonably low-priced housing, flats and hostels to restore and maintain a balance in the city or town which is the home, as well as the work-place, of a community.

London's Covent Garden area is of particular relevance in this context. Since the decision to remove the fruit and vegetable market, proposals have come forward for comprehensive development schemes involving tall blocks of offices, hotels and flats, a massive shopping complex, a conference centre, buildings for cultural uses, and major traffic routes. Sites are being acquired and assembled. But the district as it is, with its shabby but genuine eighteenth-century character and its eighty-two listed buildings (plus many more that merit listing), accommodates a tremendous diversity of activities. It has the Royal Opera House and several theatres. It has many firms (some small and only marginally economic) of publishers, engravers, graphic designers and printers, tailors, dressmakers and shoemakers (including one long-established ballet-shoe maker), booksellers, bookbinders, frame-makers and other craft workshops, charitable organizations and small restaurants and pubs; and it houses many families whose home it has been for generations. Few of these would wish, or could afford, to take new premises at what would inevitably be much higher rents.

Comprehensive redevelopment would mean not only severe problems with rehousing and reinstatement of businesses (many of which would probably cease to operate anywhere else); it would also cause the break-up of a community and the loss of a colourful and historic facet of London's character. Economics may dictate high-density redevelopment of selected sites along the edges of the area, but humanity should put a brake on interference with the mature fabric of the inner part, which cries out for conservation and sensitive redevelopment on a modest scale.

Traffic represents another, and increasing, threat to the townscapes of the future. The remedies of road networks and environmental areas advanced in the Buchanan Report are proving exceedingly costly and seem unlikely to be implemented in any but the most pressing situations for years to come. The remedy of 'traffic management' is a mixed bag of blunt instruments (carriageway-widenings here and there, the easing of curves and junctions, the introduction of one-way systems and ever more signs) and of refined instruments which expose and quantify electronically, but do not solve, the problems of flow. The combination goes some way towards accommodating and speeding the movement of traffic, but the interests of townscape would be better served by reducing and slowing down the traffic which at present invades sensitive urban areas.

Activities in buildings attract traffic, but some attract much more than others. The problem would begin to solve itself if activities that attract large amounts of traffic could be segregated from those that generate much less. Department stores, multiples, food supermarkets and large self-service retailers have many employees and attract a great many customers. They thrive on accessibility and rely on wide roads to accommodate buses and to give access to car parks for shoppers, service areas where lorries and vans unload and load, and the very large spaces needed for the huge 'warehouses on wheels' that replenish grocery supermarkets. Although large-scale retailing premises need a central-area location, they are inappropriate in a historic core or Conservation Area with a pattern of small streets and passageways and a good stock of historic buildings. If large-scale retailing invades, or wishes to expand in, such an area, it will inevitably cause drastic alterations to the fabric by way of street-widenings, service areas and parking space. It will also cause damage to historic buildings, which will be gutted at ground level [73] in order to provide wide areas of unencumbered floorspace, or total loss of such buildings by demolition and rebuilding.

If, however, the large-scale retailers could be encouraged to expand or develop in parts of central areas which are not so sensitive, and where accessibility and parking can be more easily improved, historic cores could be reserved for the kinds of trade that do not attract concentrations of shoppers and do not depend upon large parking areas close at hand. Small buildings of historic or architectural quality are well suited to businesses which do not need extensive window-display space and can make use of upper floors. These include jewellers, antique dealers, bookshops, bespoke tailors, milliners, photographers' studios, teashops and restaurants.

Planning control does not yet extend to deciding what kinds of retail use shall and shall not be permitted in particular premises. If a building of architectural or historic interest is already in use as a shop, planning control cannot prevent its being used for a different retail trade, apart from those specified in the Use Classes Order.* Nor can planning powers prevent 'modernization', for example by the replacement of a historic shop-front. It is open to an owner to remove an unlisted period shop-front and substitute, for instance, plate-glass windows and doors, framed in polished and anodized aluminium, with waist-rails and stallriser panels, glass louvres, foldaway blinds and illuminated transom signs and fascias. This, though acceptable in a modern building in a modern setting, would be crudely discordant in a good period building.

Alterations of this kind have taken place more frequently in recent times, especially among unostentatious, well-mannered Victorian and Edwardian shop-fronts. There are two reasons. First, new methods of retailing, especially self-service, have made display-windows less important or quite unnecessary: large plate-glass windows and doors display the entire shop rather than a small selection of its merchandise. Second, a bright 'new look' shop-front almost invariably brings an immediate increase in trade. Maintaining the historic fabric and the integrity of good buildings in central business districts is thus a constant challenge for local planning authorities. Fortunately, the majority of owners of 'listed' buildings (such as those shown in 10, 12, 19, 24 and 25) are aware of the merit of their properties and take

* Under this order planning consent may be required for a change of use to 'a shop for the sale of hot food, a tripe shop, a shop for the sale of pet animals and birds, a cats'-meat shop, or a shop for the sale of motor vehicles'.

good care of them. But the profit to be gained from 'modernizing', or combining adjacent buildings to form larger areas of ground-floorspace, is an ever-present incentive for change.

When striving to maintain the historic fabric of a central core, whether or not a conservation area, a planning authority may be able to withstand pressures for redevelopment by announcing and adhering to determined negative measures. If the authority resolves not to widen streets, not to ease street curves and junctions, not to improve access to the rear of business premises, and not to provide increased car parking for shoppers or office workers, then retail traders who rely upon ready accessibility for shoppers *en masse* and enterprises whose employees are numbered in hundreds rather than dozens will be discouraged from entering or expanding in the locality and will have to seek alternative locations. To offset the effect of these negative measures the planning authority would need to take positive steps to ensure that suitable alternative locations were available for such large-scale developments.

To safeguard the integrity of historic buildings in such a location, the means available are less effective. The planning authority can publish its criteria (as discussed at the end of Chapter 8) for assessing applications for 'development', including alteration. Prospective developers will be made aware of the criteria and will be encouraged to abide by them. Applications that fail to observe them, in the spirit or the letter, can then be rejected, or delayed while acceptable alternatives are discussed. The support of local civic societies and the local press can also be enlisted to gauge the strength of public opinion for or against the proposed changes. Nevertheless if an owner is determined to press on with his proposals (provided that they do not involve demolition) and will go to appeal, the planning system as operated at political level by the Department of the Environment and local planning authorities is likely to favour him in the long run.

Private owners are not the only offenders in the destruction of historic townscapes. Town councils are equally culpable, if not more so. In conjunction with property developers and building firms, some councils have acquiesced in the comprehensive destruction that precedes comprehensive redevelopment. They have proposed, and often implemented, the construction of inner ring roads that caused great swathes of destruction, erasing not only buildings of character but also the delicate patterns of intimate streets and lanes and passages and sudden squares designed for man on his feet, and no less suitable for the purpose today. They have lost no time in obtaining ministerial consent for the demolition of any listed buildings that stood in the way of redevelopment. They have ridden roughshod over public opinion as expressed by local civic societies and individuals. The boorish destruction that befell much of Worcester and Lincoln, and many other places, is still at work.

A recent case is Carlisle, whose council has already launched the construction of an inner ring road by destroying its finest residential street. In partnership with a building firm, it now intends to impose a reinforced-concrete shopping precinct, to contain four big stores, fifty-nine shops, roof-top parking, offices and a discothèque. This will wipe out much of the town centre, which has small period shop-fronts clustered around a modestly elegant town hall of 1717, and pleasant little cobbled lanes behind the main shopping frontages. No thought seems to have been given to the alternative of selective redevelopment along existing streets and lanes, which would retain the original fabric and identity.

Carlisle's mayor is reported[1] to have said: 'Personally I'm sick and tired of people going on about the period shop-fronts. I see no interest in them. Architecturally they leave me cold.' If this reflects the view of his council, it strengthens the case advanced by the Council for British Archaeology* that conservation of historic cities and towns is too important to be left to local councils, especially those which lack understanding of their heritage or have no specialist staff to advise them. The Department of the Environment's Circular 46/73[2] draws attention to the possibility of sharing specialist teams experienced in conservation among groups of district authorities; but it will require a watchful eye in the Department of the Environment to ensure that conservation policies are pursued with more than lip-service.

The future of townscapes, especially in towns of architectural or historic interest, is closely connected with the economic viability of

See Chapter 5, p. 132.

219

Townscapes

their fabric and buildings. Obviously, no town can survive for long unless its inhabitants, its ratepayers, can make a living there. Only exceptionally do towns subsist as museum pieces or as predominantly tourist attractions. Williamsburg, Virginia, and Georgetown in the Rockies (already mentioned), Carcassonne fortress in France and Rothenburg in Germany are some that come to mind; Culross in Scotland is a borderline example. If an urban fabric is to be maintained as the home of a permanent and employed population, as well as for the benefit of visitors and tourists, it will be necessary from time to time to replace inefficient old buildings with efficient new ones, while continuing to maintain most of the other old buildings in uses that are at least self-financing.

A policy for conservation must embrace both preservation and change. Both may be achieved by bargaining between the planning authority and the owner. For example, the planning authority may be able to secure retention of the front part of an architecturally interesting building by consenting to substantial additional new accommodation at the rear. Or it may agree to allow changes of use from residential to commercial or other, so that large houses no longer suitable for single-family occupation and not convenient for subdivision into flats can be adapted to house offices or institutions.

Protagonists of conservation sometimes take the view that buildings of architectural or historic interest should be shielded from market forces and protected for their own sake. Owners and prospective developers usually take the opposing view that conservation must always be self-financing. Studies of town development in history show that the latter view has normally prevailed. With few exceptions, notably cathedrals, churches and castles, buildings of non-monumental character that survived into the twentieth century did so because of their intrinsic merit and usefulness rather than by official protection. But demands for more concentrated use of space in central areas, in the post-war years in particular, made and continue to make increasing threats to the survivors. Their continued existence must depend upon cooperation from private owners who, in general, require financial recompense if they are to forgo financially attractive alternatives.

The present situation is that owners who are refused listed-building consent are left with the responsibility of maintaining their building in good use and repair. This is somewhat harsh if the income produced is scarcely adequate to meet higher-than-normal costs of maintenance and is very far below that which could be derived from redevelopment. There seems to be a good case for allowing some relief from rates to owners who must continue to meet such expenses.

The financial decision whether to conserve or redevelop is, however, seldom a decision between readily comparable alternatives. In the case of a terrace of houses, the arguments for conservation might be that the buildings have architectural merit; that the capital value of their sound foundations, walls, roofs and interior construction is retained; and that modernization can be carried out at reasonable cost. The arguments against conservation might be that redevelopment would produce accommodation of more convenient size and shape; that economies could be effected by the use of standardized components; and that maintenance costs would be lower than for rehabilitated property. The factor that often clinches the argument, however, is that planning consent for redevelopment almost invariably means that more units of accommodation can be provided than were there before, thus affording greater return on investment. In the case of shops and offices, the profitability of redevelopment compared with conservation would be even greater.

Planning control could do much to discourage proposals for redevelopment in areas where buildings of architectural interest abound by restricting the quota of accommodation to no more than is there at present, thereby removing the major incentive to investment for profit. If such a restriction were considered unreasonable, the alternative would be to award the owner a grant from public funds to cover the difference between unprofitable and modestly profitable restoration and enhancement. The use of conservation grants[3] goes some way towards resolving this difficulty.

In contemplating the future for townscapes, emphasis has been laid on conservation because people are familiar with the townscape as it is; they can study proposals that may bring significant change, can formulate views and can make them known to the planning authority and, if need be, to the Inspector at a local inquiry. But conservation, in the sense of retaining and modifying old buildings, is only half the battle for townscapes: the equally necessary other half is the replacement of old urban fabric with new. In the overall campaign against the enemy – ugly, inhuman, unhealthy and dangerous urban environment – the architectural profession must take a commanding role.

Over the past quarter of a century or so, the architect seems to have lost some of the confidence of 'the troops' – the people who support him by using and paying for, directly or indirectly, his additions to the townscape. He seems to have been engaged in private battles: seeking a new architectural vernacular for new materials, new methods of construction and new dimensions of giantism; trying to get the best possible results out of instructions from unimaginative or illiberal clients; seeking to attain originality and ingenuity in the face of prosaic planning controls and rigid building regulations; and sometimes seeking to impress fellow-architects with startling buildings that bear little relation to their surroundings. In the midst of such preoccupations the architect has rarely come up with buildings that are welcome additions to the townscape, and he seems unconcerned that people may be affronted by ill-assorted or dreary newcomers (like those which flank Saffron Walden's Post Office [79]).

Short of drastic change in the present planning and building controls, it is probable that proposals for most new buildings will continue to be submitted by non-architects. Blame for shortcomings in townscape will not therefore lie entirely with architects, other than those whose duty it is to advise local planning authorities on the granting of planning consents. The architectural profession is likely to command in three principal spheres: redevelopment of key sites in city centres; design of one-off jobs for special purposes; and design of dwelling-types for use in large-scale schemes for public or private developers. The quality of design and finish that architects achieve in these areas will surely influence the standard of work among other building developers.

What does the general public expect of architects shaping the townscapes of the future? Lay people who care about townscape expect that new buildings in the High Street, the market place and other conspicuous and frequented places will appear not as exotic intruders but as good neighbours, respecting existing character where desirable and adhering to, even improving upon, the planning authority's criteria for the locality. Lay people also look to the profession to secure a better environment for their buildings: to influence developer-clients to allocate sufficient space and resources to finish a job properly. The high standard of finish must apply not only to the buildings but to boundary walls, bollards, lighting, floorscape and planting as well; it should manifest professional attention to all details of the composition, rather than the application of 'architectural ivy' to conceal deficiencies.

Some contemporary architects have done much to bring about a reawakening to pride of place, whether in city centres, new and expanded towns, municipal extensions, or villages. They have stimulated growing awareness of the need to design buildings of human scale, to abandon the fine Corbusian frenzy of gigantic units assembled in vastly comprehensive array, as exemplified in the fearsome Bijlmermeer housing estate south-east of Amsterdam. The present emphasis is more on large-scale forms that seek to reconcile high densities with low-rise buildings and intensive land use with increased privacy and private open space, and on smaller-scale and selective redevelopment as opposed to 'clean sweep and build afresh'. These are good signs. Even better would be signs that architects are seeking to reassure the many lay people who are anxious to conserve buildings because they are distrustful of what might replace them: who prefer to

> ... keep a-hold of Nurse
> For fear of finding something worse.

Success for architects on that front would indeed augur well for townscapes.

Appendix I
Reading Townscape Survey

This pilot survey in Reading was devised by the author, and carried out on two consecutive days in June 1973 by second-year undergraduates in the Department of Land Management and Development at Reading University.[1]

Reading is rich in historical associations, but unusually poor in tangible evidence of them. Its Roman and Saxon existence has no visible remains. The huge Cluniac Abbey, founded in 1121 by Henry I, has lain in ruin for more than four centuries. Its medieval prosperity, derived largely from cloth, is dimly reflected in the pitifully few surviving buildings of the period. Its elegant eighteenth-century and Regency townscape is represented by a fair, though diminishing, number of individual buildings and groups; the houses are mostly well-maintained, but shops of the period have often been spoilt by large, modern display-windows and unsightly fascias and advertisements, and some houses have deteriorated as a result of conversion to office or other non-residential use.

The greater part of the inherited townscape is representative of the vigorously successful Victorian period, when much of the wealth from light industries, brewing, biscuit-making, trade in seeds and other activities was invested in buildings that together composed a solid and varied fabric. Some notable churches (one by Pugin), a town hall (by Waterhouse) with a tower providing a dominating focal point, other impressive municipal buildings, commercial offices, shops, hotels and houses for all income levels – all embody a tradition identified less by outstanding skill in design than by the care and pride of good craftsmen using first-rate building materials, mostly of local origin.

Appendix I: Reading Townscape Survey

Buildings arising from post-war prosperity and comprehensive redevelopment are taking an increasing share of the total townscape; but office blocks, a multi-storey car park, shopping centres and blocks of flats have brought few proud new features in skyline or townscape.

Lack of official interest in the mounting losses from the Victorian and earlier heritages is much in evidence; it can soon be discovered on a walk in the central area with, as guide books, the Ministry's provisional list of 'Buildings of Special Architectural or Historic Interest', dated 1946, and the approved list of 1957. A few examples: Finch's Buildings in Hosier Street (owned by Reading Corporation), rated Grade II, drew the additional comment from the Inspectors: 'The whole group is picturesque and, in part, a rare example of medieval buildings remaining in Reading'. They were destroyed to give space for rear access to a new shopping precinct. Numbers 16 and 17 Friar Street (Grade II), with the Inspectors' accolade 'a very fine example of the period (early C. 18); should be preserved', were also destroyed for redevelopment. Number 22 The Market Place (Grade II, c. 1810, the former Town Serjeant's House), owned by the corporation and capable of beneficial use, was neglected for some years and destroyed in 1973 in furtherance of the comprehensive redevelopment plan. The same fate befell number 22 The Forbury, an exceptionally fine late-seventeenth-century house, Greyfriars Vicarage (by Sir John Soane) and many other buildings of seventeenth- and eighteenth-century date.

The Ministry's lists unfortunately make practically no mention of buildings later than 1840, apart from the Town Hall, the County Gaol and a pair of shops. Yet this is the period that gave the town its strong Victorian character, and from which chunks are readily sacrificed whenever developers choose a site for a profitable venture.

The Survey aimed to discover something of Reading townspeople's attitudes to their changing environment.

The interviewers, stationed in pairs at selected locations in the Market Place and along shopping streets where recent changes had taken place, invited passers-by to give answers to a questionnaire, shown overleaf with the main results inserted. Of 771 people

225

Townscapes

Students of Land Management & Development at the University have noticed many changes in the appearance of the town, especially its central area, and would like to know what Reading people feel about these changes.

1. Do you visit Reading main shopping streets regularly?

M	2	4	6
F	2	4	6
Daily			
Weekly			
Monthly			

2. Which of these streets, if any, do you think is most typical of Reading's 'character':

   (a) Broad Street   (b) Queen Victoria Street
   (c) Castle Street   (d) Friar Street
   (e) London Street   (f) Gun Street?

a	b	c
d	e	f

a 42%
b 11%
d 18%

3. Have you noticed Victorian buildings in Reading's main streets (e.g. Art Gallery; Elephant Hotel and Westminster Bank in the Market Place; Athenaeum and Nicholas in Friar Street)? Do you think that they are:

   (a) attractive   (b) ugly
   (c) indifferent?

82%   16%

YES/NO	

57%   14%   24%

a	b	c

4. Do you think that the outsides of these buildings are:

   (a) attractive   (b) ugly
   (c) indifferent?

   Sainsbury's (Friar Street)
   Marks & Spencer (Broad Street)
   Sutton's (Market Place)
   The Butts Shopping Centre*

a	b	c
a	b	c
a	b	c
a	b	c
a	b	c

*41%   37%   20%

Appendix I: Reading Townscape Survey

5. (i) Do you remember the curved, stone-faced building, on the corner of the Market Place leading into the Forbury, that was demolished earlier this year?

65%   29%

YES/NO

(ii) Do you know that the Council agreed in 1965 to a plan that involves removal of most of the old buildings in the Market Place?

29%   71%

YES/NO

(iii) Would you like to see **all** the old buildings replaced with new ones in the same style as Market Place House (next to the Electricity Showrooms)?

18%   81%

YES/NO

54%   46%

6. (i) Do you know that the Town Hall is to be demolished and its site redeveloped to help pay for the new Town Hall?

YES/NO

(ii) Do you support this action?

YES/NO

35%   60%

(iii) Would you be prepared to pay a little more in rates to keep the present Town Hall for community uses?

YES/NO

41·36%   41·51%

7. Do you think that the Council should do more to encourage:

    (a) keeping main street façades largely unaltered but modernizing interiors, or
    (b) placing new buildings side-by-side with the best of the old ones, or
    (c) redeveloping streets on a large scale in modern styles, as, e.g., the Butts Shopping Centre?

a	45%
b	36%
c	15%

8. Have you heard of the Reading Civic Society?
    Would you like information about its work?

32% | YES/NO | 65%

36% | YES/NO | 55%

approached, 652 made a positive response, giving 10–15 minutes of their time. The sex and age-group of those questioned were recorded, the latter categorized as young, middle-aged or elderly. (These are denoted on the questionnaire by the numbers 2, 4 and 6, standing for 'about 20', 'about 40' and 'about 60'.) Each group was well represented, but the young (38 per cent) and middle-aged (37 per cent) were rather more in evidence than the elderly (25 per cent).

The questions of a general nature sought to discover whether people thought that Reading's central area had 'character' and, if so, with what period that character was mostly associated. This somewhat abstract question was made more tangible by reference to three streets (Broad Street, Friar Street and Queen Victoria Street) of predominantly Victorian character, two (London Street and Castle Street) which are predominantly Georgian, and one (Gun Street) which contains a mixture of both. Although the first reaction from some of the respondents was doubt that Reading had 'character' of any kind, opinion held Broad Street (with 42 per cent) to be most typical, followed by Friar Street (18 per cent) and Queen Victoria Street (11 per cent). Thus the predominantly Victorian streets, with modern buildings inserted here and there, seemed to be thought the most evocative of Reading's identity.

Response to question 3 showed that 82 per cent had noticed the Victorian buildings cited in the questionnaire, 16 per cent had not, and 2 per cent seemed uncertain whether they were Victorian. As to whether these buildings were attractive, 57 per cent thought they were, 14 per cent thought them ugly, and 24 per cent thought them indifferent. Opinions about the elevations of the four prominent modern buildings cited in question 4 were mostly that they were indifferent. The only exception was the Butts Shopping Centre, thought attractive by 41 per cent, ugly by 37 per cent and indifferent by 20 per cent.

The questions concerned with particular issues elicited clear-cut replies. 65 per cent remembered, and 29 per cent did not remember, the curved, stone-faced building, number 22 Market Place, which had been demolished a few months previously. Only 29 per cent were aware (with 71 per cent unaware) of the plan which involved removing most of the old buildings flanking the Market Place and substituting structures of uniform elevation. Preference for retaining existing buildings was decisively stated: 81 per cent for retention, 18 per cent for rebuilding and 1 per cent with no opinion.

Answers to question 6 concerning the Town Hall showed that 54 per cent were aware and 46 per cent unaware of the council's intention not to retain it. 60 per cent favoured retention, 35 per cent did not, and 5 per cent were undecided. If it came to making a small financial sacrifice ('a little more on the rates') for its preservation, 41·36 per cent were willing, 41·51 per cent were not, and 17·13 per cent were undecided.

Question 7 sought to discover whether people preferred to see as few changes as possible in main streets, to see new buildings side-by-side with old ones, or to see widespread clearance and redevelopment in modern styles. It produced a majority (45 per cent) in favour of keeping street façades largely unaltered but with interiors adapted and modernized for new uses. The second preference (36 per cent) was for placing modern buildings beside the best of the old so as to achieve a mixture of periods and styles, and the least-preferred (15 per cent) alternative was comprehensive redevelopment which necessarily involved comprehensive clearance of existing townscape.

Question 8 was included at the request of Reading Civic Society's committee, which wished to test the extent of public interest in and potential support for its work. The response proved rather discouraging for the Society. 32 per cent had heard of it, 65 per cent had not, and 3 per cent expressed uncertainty. 36 per cent said they would like more information about the Society's work, 55 per cent said they would not, and 9 per cent were undecided. This suggested that, while people are willing to discuss and express views and wishes, they are less willing to become involved in working towards their realization.

Appendix II
Notes on financing of conservation

Grants for implementing conservation are available from central government in three forms: from Historic Buildings Councils; via local authorities under the Local Authorities (Historic Buildings) Act, 1962; and as 'revolving funds'.

A total of £1½ million annually is put at the disposal of the Historic Buildings Councils for the repair and maintenance of individual buildings of outstanding architectural and historic importance (for instance, 'stately homes'), for 'Town Schemes' sponsored jointly by the Department of the Environment and local authorities, and for conservation grants to enhance the character and appearance of outstanding Conservation Areas. Grants may be supplied for the improvement of buildings, listed or not, especially those in groups such as terraces, whole streets, squares, market places, and so on, and other features which add to the quality of the area, for example, cobbles, paving, and street-lighting. The government pays part of the cost, and owners and the local authority the remainder, in varying proportions.

Under the Local Authorities (Historic Buildings) Act, 1962, local authorities may obtain government grants towards the repair and maintenance of historic buildings, listed or otherwise, of high quality but not necessarily of outstanding importance. The grants may be used for buildings owned by the local authorities, or allocated to private owners or the National Trust.

The revolving-fund method is used by local authorities and the many building trusts, conservation trusts, improvement trusts and similar bodies. (An examination of the method was published by the Civic Trust in its pamphlet 'Financing the Preservation of Old Buildings' in 1971.) The Buckinghamshire £100,000 Scheme is a recent example. The county council's policy is to purchase buildings of outstanding architectural or historic interest from owners who cannot afford to undertake the necessary repairs and cannot find a purchaser able and willing to do so. The council then renovates the building and sells it, recouping the outlay on purchase and capital works. Operations are always limited to the outlay of £100,000 at any one time. It is not the council's intention to accumulate property, but to restore it and pass it on. It has not used powers of compulsory purchase, but has successfully dealt with several buildings with a comfortable excess of receipts over expenditure. The Scheme has also stimulated private developers to undertake conservation of hitherto umpromising properties.

The National Trust in Scotland operates the revolving-fund system for its Little Houses Improvement Scheme. The Trust purchases small buildings of good vernacular architecture; it then sells them to private purchasers who undertake to restore them to the Trust's specifications, or to other purchasers after restoration by the Trust's own craftsmen. In either case the Trust retains control over the initial restoration and, through covenants, over future maintenance or alterations. The size of the fund available at the start of the scheme had quadrupled a decade later, and the larger it gets the more properties can be purchased and renewed.

References

Chapter 1

1. A. E. Smailes, *Geography of Towns* (Hutchinson, 1953, 1966; available in paperback)
2. Gerald Burke, *Towns in the Making* (Edward Arnold, 1971)
3. Alect Clifton-Taylor, *The Pattern of English Building* (Faber, new edn, 1972)
4. R. M. Robbins, *Middlesex* (Collins, 1953)
5. W. G. Hoskins, *The Making of the English Landscape* (Penguin, 1970)
6. Colin Buchanan, *et al.*, *Traffic in Towns* (HMSO, 1963; shorter version in Penguin edn, 1963)

Chapter 2

1. M. W. Beresford, *New Towns of the Middle Ages* (Lutterworth, 1967)
2. Gerald Burke, *Towns in the Making* (Edward Arnold, 1971)
3. Camillo Sitte, *City Planning According to Artistic Principles* (1889, tr. G. R. Collins, Random House, 1965)
4. Kurt Rowland, *The Shape of Towns* (Ginn, 1966)
5. e.g. L. B. Alberti, *The Architecture of Leon Battista Alberte*, (tr. James Leoni, Thomas Edlin, 1726)
6. Ralph Dutton, *The English Garden* (Batsford, 1967)
7. J. C. Loudon, *Encyclopaedia of Gardening* (Longman, Rees, Orme, Brown, Green & Longman, 1835)
8. Paul Lavedan, *Histoire de l'urbanisme, Renaissance et temps modernes* (Laureus, Paris, 1941)
9. Gerald Burke, *The Making of Dutch Towns* (Cleaver-Hume, 1956)
10. John Summerson, *Architecture in Britain 1530–1830* (Penguin, 1963)
11. John Summerson, *Inigo Jones* (Penguin, 1966)
12. John Summerson, *Georgian London* (Pleiades Press, 1945)
13. Walter Ison, *The Georgian Buildings of Bath from 1700 to 1830* (Faber, 1948)

14. A. J. Youngson, *The Making of Classical Edinburgh* (Edinburgh University Press, 1966)
15. Camillo Sitte, op. cit.
16. Raymond Unwin, *Town Planning in Practice* (Benn, second edn, 1911)

Chapter 3

1. Quotation from Canon Parkinson in Asa Briggs, *Victorian Cities* (Penguin, 1971)
2. A. W. N. Pugin, *Contrasts* (Leicester University Press, 1969)
3. Quotations from Whitburn, P. R., 'Retailing and the Conservation of Historic Centres' (unpublished thesis, University of London, 1972)
5. Quotation from journals of 1854 in Hermione Hobhouse, *Thomas Cubitt, Master Builder* (Macmillan, 1971)
6. H.-R. Hitchcock, *Architecture and Twentieth Centuries* (Penguin, 1955)
7. quotation Banister Fletcher, *A History of Architecture by the Comparative Method* (Athlone Press, seventeenth edn, 1961)
8. ibid.
9. Nikolaus Pevsner, *London 1: Except the Cities of London and Westminster*, (Penguin, 1952)
10. Shankland Cox & Associates, New Hampstead Garden Suburb Trust Ltd, *Report*, 1972

Chapter 4

1. J. M. Richards, *An Introduction to Modern Architecture* (Penguin, 1940)
2. William Holford, *The Built Environment, Its Creation, Motivations and Control* (Tavistock Pamphlet No. 11, The Tavistock Lecture, 1964)
3. Quotation from Frederick Gibberd, in article by John Chisholm in the *Daily Telegraph*, 7 March, 1970
4. J. M. Richards, 'The Hollow Victory: 1932–72' (RIBA Annual Discourse, 1972)
5. BSI Code of Practice 1004
6. Stephen Plowden, *Traffic Against Towns* (André Deutsch, 1972)
7. David Crawford, 'Straitjacket' (*Architectural Review*, October 1973, pp. 228–38)

Townscapes

Chapter 5

1. M. R. G. Conzen, 'The Use of Town Plans', in H. J. Dyos, ed., *The Study of Urban History* (Arnold, 1968), and *Alnwick, Northumberland, A Study in Town Plan Analysis* (George Philip & Son Ltd, 1960)
2. G. H. Martin, 'The Town as a Palimpsest' in Dyos, op. cit.
3. CBA Urban Research Committee, *The Erosion of History* (Council for British Archaeology, 1972)
4. H.-R. Hitchcock, *Architecture: Nineteenth and Twentieth Centuries* (Penguin, 1955)
5. Hermione Hobhouse, *Lost London* (Macmillan, 1971)
6. Department of the Environment, *New Life for Old Buildings* (HMSO, 1971)
7. Civic Trust, *Conservation in Action* (1972)
8. Ministry of Housing and Local Government, Preservation Policy Group (HMSO, 1970)
9. Studies in Conservation: Colin Buchanan & Partners, *Bath* (HMSO, 1968); Donald Insall & Associates, *Chester* (HMSO, 1968); G. S. Burrows, *Chichester* (HMSO, 1968); Lord Esher, *York* (HMSO, 1968)
10. As 9. Also, Department of the Environment, *New Life for Historic Areas* (HMSO, 1972); Department of the Environment, *How do you want to live?* (Report of the Working Party on the Human Habitat, UN Conference on the Human Environment, Stockholm, 1972; HMSO)
11. Civic Trust, *The First Three Years* (Report by the Trustees, 1960)

Chapter 6

1. Tony Aldous, *Battle for the Environment* (Fontana, 1972)
2. L. Rainwater, *Behind Ghetto Walls* (Penguin, 1971)
3. Ministry of Housing and Local Government, *The Deeplish Study: Improvement Possibilities in a District of Rochdale* (HMSO, 1966)
4. Sherban Cantacuzino, review article in *Architectural Review*, Vol. CLIV No. 918, August 1973
5. Ministry of Town and Country Planning, Final Report of the New Towns Committee (Cmd 6759, HMSO, 1946)

Chapter 7

1. George Dolony, Review of the Development Control System, Final Report to the Department of the Environment (HMSO, 1975)
2. Design Council, *Street Furniture Catalogue* (published periodically)
3. Civic Trust, *Pride of Place* (1972)
4. Kevin Lynch, *The Image of the City* (MIT Press, 1960)
5. B. Goodey, 'Perception of the Environment' (Occasional Paper No. 17, CES, University of Birmingham, 1973)
6. Gordon Cullen, *Notation* (Alcan Industries, 1968)
7. Civic Trust for the North West, *Environmental Quality – A Measuring System* (1971)

Chapter 8

1. A. W. N. Pugin, *Contrasts* (Leicester University Press, 1969)
2. GLC, *Greater London Development Plan, Report of Studies* (p. 267)
3. GLC, op. cit., Chapter 8.
4. George Dobry, Review of the Development Control System, Interim Report to the Department of the Environment (HMSO, 1974), para. 4.7
5. City of Westminster Development Plan, Summary Paper S2 (1972)
6. City of Westminster Development Plan Draft of Policy Paper P1 (1972)
7. George Dobry, Review of the Development Control System, Final Report to he Department of the Environment (HMSO, 1975)

Chapter 9

1. For procedure and a check-list for organising and implementing a scheme of improvement see *Pride of Place* (Civic Trust, 1972)
2. Anthony Swaine, *Faversham Conserved* (Kent County Council, 1969)
3. *Wonen en Werken in een Restauratiepabd* (pamphlet, undated, c. 1973)
4. Theo Hartmann, *Der Churer Marktplatz* (Chur Municipality, 1968)
5. op. cit, p. 19
6. op. cit., pp. 21 and 23
7. National Planning Commission, *The Proposed Comprehensive Plan for*

the National Capital (US Government Printing Office, Washington DC, 1967)

8. Larimer Square Associates, *Larimer Square Market Analysis* (1974)
9. Commended in the Royal Institution of Chartered Surveyors/*The Times* Conservation Awards, 1974.
10. Data kindly supplied by the Royal Swedish Embassy, London, and officials in Stockholm.
11. City of Coventry, *Spon Street Townscape Scheme* (1967)
12. F. W. B. Charles, *The Structural Restoration and Re-erection of Ancient Timber-framed Buildings in Coventry* (unpublished paper, September 1972)
13. F. W. B. Charles, op. cit.

Chapter 10

1. *Sunday Times*, 3 March 1974
2. Department of the Environment, *Conservation and Preservation, Local Government Act, 1972* (Circular 46/73, HMSO)
3. Civic Trust, *Financing and Preservation of Old Buildings* (1971). See also Appendix II.

Appendix I

1. Gerald Burke, 'Do Residents Care Much About Reading?', *Built Environment*, March 1974

Further reading

Nikolaus Pevsner, *The Buildings of England* (Penguin, 46 volumes, 1951–74)

Thomas Sharp, *Town and Townscape* (John Murray (Publishers) Ltd, 1968)

Gordon Cullen, *Townscape* (Architectural Press, 1961)

Ewart Johns, *British Townscape* (Arnold, 1965)

R. Worskett, *The Characters of Towns* (Architectural Press, 1969)

S. E. Rasmussen, *Towns and Buildings* (Liverpool University Press, 1951)

See also comprehensive reading-lists in R. Worskett, op. cit., and Civic Trust Library.

Index

Numbers in italics are page-numbers of illustrations.

Index

Index

242

Index

Index